USING
iphone®

Covers iPhone 3G, 3GS, and 4 running iOS 4

Paul McFedries

Using iPhone®

Cover iPhone 3G, 3GS, and 4 running IOS4

Copyright © 2011 by Pearson Education, Inc.

ISBN-13: 978-0-7897-4525-5

ISBN-10: 0-7897-4525-9

Library of Congress Cataloging-in-Publication data is on file.

Printed in the United States of America

First Printing: September 2010

Trademarks

All terms mentioned in this book that are known to be trademarks or service marks have been appropriately capitalized. Que Publishing cannot attest to the accuracy of this information. Use of a term in this book should not be regarded as affecting the validity of any trademark or service mark.

Mac OS and Snow Leopard are registered trademarks of Apple Inc.

Warning and Disclaimer

Bulk Sales

Que Publishing offers excellent discounts on this book when ordered in quantity for bulk purchases or special sales. For more information, please contact

U.S. Corporate and Government Sales
1-800-382-3419
corpsales@pearsontechgroup.com

For sales outside of the U.S., please contact

International Sales
international@pearson.com

Associate Publisher
Greg Wiegand

Acquisitions Editor
Laura Norman

Development Editor
Dan Workman

Managing Editor
Sandra Schroeder

Project Editor
Mandie Frank

Copy Editor
Keith Cline

Indexer
Tim Wright

Proofreader
Megan Wade

Technical Editor
Christian Kenyeres

Publishing Coordinator
Cindy Teeters

Book Designer
Anne Jones

Cover Designer
Anna Stingley

Multimedia Developer
John Herrin

Compositor
Mark Shirar

Contents at a Glance

Audio/Video Files Table of Contents

To register this product and gain access to audio and video files, go to www.informit.com/register and sign in and enter the ISBN. After you register the product, a link to the additional content will be listed on your Account page, under Registered Products.

Table of Contents

About the Author

Paul McFedries is an iPhone expert and full-time technical writer. Paul has been authoring computer books since 1991 and has more than 70 books to his credit, which combined have sold more than 3 million copies worldwide. His titles include the Que Publishing books *USING the Microsoft Office Web Apps, Formulas and Functions with Microsoft Excel 2010; Tricks of the Microsoft Office 2007 Gurus*; and *Tweak It and Freak It: A Killer Guide to Making Windows Run Your Way*, as well as the Sams Publishing book *Windows 7 Unleashed*. Paul is also the proprietor of Word Spy (http://www.wordspy.com), a website devoted to *lexpionage*, the sleuthing of new words and phrases that have entered the English language. Please drop by Paul's personal website at http://www.mcfedries.com or follow Paul on Twitter at twitter.com/paulmcf.

Dedication

This book is dedicated to the loving memory of Gypsy, the Best Dog Ever.

Acknowledgments

If you reread your work, you can find on rereading a great deal of repetition can be avoided by rereading and editing.

—William Safire

In the fast-paced world of computer book writing, where deadlines come whooshing at you at alarming speeds and with dismaying regularity, rereading a manuscript is a luxury reserved only for those who have figured out how to live a 36-hour day. Fortunately, every computer book does get reread[md]not once, not twice, but many times. I speak, of course, not of the diligence of this book's author, but of the yeoman work done by this book's many and various editors, those sharp-eyed, red-pencil-wielding worthies whose job it is to make a book's author look good. Near the front of the book you'll find a long list of the hard-working professionals whose fingers made it into this particular paper pie. However, there are a few folks I worked with directly, and I'd like to single them out for extra credit. A big, heaping helping of thanks goes out to Acquisitions Editor Laura Norman, Development Editor Dan Workman, Project Editor Mandie Frank, Copy Editor Keith Kline, and Technical Editor Christian Kenyeres. Great work, everyone!

We Want to Hear from You!

As the reader of this book, *you* are our most important critic and commentator. We value your opinion and want to know what we're doing right, what we could do better, what areas you'd like to see us publish in, and any other words of wisdom you're willing to pass our way.

As an associate publisher for Que Publishing, I welcome your comments. You can email or write me directly to let me know what you did or didn't like about this book—as well as what we can do to make our books better.

Please note that I cannot help you with technical problems related to the topic of this book. We do have a User Services group, however, where I will forward specific technical questions related to the book.

When you write, please be sure to include this book's title and author as well as your name, email address, and phone number. I will carefully review your comments and share them with the author and editors who worked on the book.

Email: feedback@quepublishing.com

Mail: Greg Wiegand
Associate Publisher
Que Publishing
800 East 96th Street
Indianapolis, IN 46240 USA

Reader Services

Visit our website and register this book at http://quepublishing.com/using for convenient access to any updates, downloads, or errata that might be available for this book.

Introduction

The iPhone is a success not because tens of millions of them have been sold (or, more accurately, not *only* because tens of millions of them have been sold; that's a lot of phones!), but because the iPhone in just a couple of years has reached the status of a cultural icon. Even people who don't care much for gadgets in general and cell phones in particular know about the iPhone. And for those of us who *do* care about gadgets, the iPhone elicits a kind of technological longing that can only be satisfied in one way: by *buying* one.

Part of the iPhone's iconic status comes from its gorgeous design and from its remarkable interface, which makes all the standard tasks—surfing, emailing, texting, scheduling, playing—easy and intuitive. But just as an attractive face or an easygoing manner can hide a personality of complexity and depth, so too does the iPhone hide many of its most useful and interesting features.

In other words, we currently have a situation where there are millions of new iPhone users, and they're all trying to figure out a gadget that, while easy to use on the surface, takes some extra effort to get the most out of.

Welcome to *USING the iPhone*

If you're a new iPhone user who, having spent a great deal of money on your phone, wants to get more out of this costly (and ongoing) investment, this book is for you. *USING the iPhone* takes you through a series of practical and useful techniques that allow you to get to know your iPhone and to incorporate the iPhone into your everyday life. The book tells you what to expect from the iPhone and what its limitations are, and it talks about best practices for using the iPhone. *USING the iPhone* teaches you not only how to use the iPhone as a phone, but also how to use it as a smartphone for surfing the Web, sending and receiving email, managing your contacts and appointments, reading eBooks, and much more. *USING the iPhone* offers you the following:

- Straightforward, to-the-point language and easy-to-follow steps

- Instructions on using all the apps that come with the iPhone, so you get a complete iPhone education

- Techniques for customizing and configuring your iPhone, so you get the most out of your investment

- Explanations of key concepts for novice users
- Real-world examples you can relate to

Using This Book

This book allows you to customize your own learning experience. The step-by-step instructions in the book give you a solid foundation in using the iPhone, while rich and varied online content, including video tutorials and audio sidebars, provide the following:

- Demonstrations of step-by-step tasks covered in the book
- Additional tips or information on a topic
- Practical advice and suggestions
- Direction for more advanced tasks not covered in the book

Here's a quick look at a few structural features designed to help you get the most out of this book:

- **Chapter roadmaps:** At the beginning of each chapter is a list of the top-level topics addressed in that chapter. This list enables you to quickly see the information the chapter contains.

- **Notes:** Notes provide additional commentary or explanation that doesn't fit neatly into the surrounding text. Notes give detailed explanations of how something works, alternative ways of performing a task, and other tidbits to get you on your way.

- **Tips:** This element gives you shortcuts, workarounds, and ways to avoid pitfalls and problems.

- **Cautions:** Every once in a while there is something that can have serious repercussions if done incorrectly (or rarely, if done at all). Cautions give you a heads-up.

- **Cross references:** Many topics are connected to other topics in various ways. Cross references help you link related information together, no matter where that information appears in the book. When another section is related to one you are reading, a cross reference directs you to a specific page in the book on which you can find the related information.

LET ME TRY IT

tasks are presented in a step-by-step sequence so you can easily follow along.

SHOW ME

video walks through tasks you've just got to see—including bonus advanced techniques.

TELL ME MORE

audio delivers practical insights straight from the experts.

Special Features

More than just a book, your USING product integrates step-by-step video tutorials and valuable audio sidebars delivered through the free Web Edition that comes with every USING book. For the price of the book, you get online access anywhere with a web connection—no books to carry, updated content as the technology changes, and the benefit of video and audio learning.

About the USING Web Edition

The Web Edition of every USING book is powered by Safari Books Online, allowing you to access the video tutorials and valuable audio sidebars. Plus, you can search the contents of the book, highlight text and attach a note to that text, print your notes and highlights in a custom summary, and cut and paste directly from Safari Books Online.

To register this product and gain access to the free Web Edition and the audio and video files, go to http://quepublishing.com/using.

This chapter introduces you to your iPhone and takes you on a tour of its features.

1

Getting to Know Your iPhone

When you look at your iPhone, you first notice its smooth, sleek design, but then you notice what might be its most remarkable feature: no buttons! Unlike your garden-variety smartphone or personal digital assistant (PDA) bristling with keys and switches and ports, your iPhone has very few physical buttons. This makes for a stylish, possibly even sexy, design, but it also leads to an obvious problem out of the box: How do you work the darn thing? This chapter solves that problem by giving you the grand tour of your iPhone. You learn about the few physical buttons on the phone, and then I show you the real heart of the iPhone, the remarkable touchscreen.

This chapter also shows you crucial iPhone tasks such as charging the battery, connecting to a wireless network, and synchronizing data between your computer and your iPhone.

Using the Home Button

The starting point for most of your iPhone excursions is the Home button, which is the circular button at the bottom of the face of the phone, as shown in Figure 1.1. The Home button has several functions, but there are two main functions: It wakes the iPhone out of standby mode, and it returns the iPhone to the Home screen.

If your iPhone is in standby mode, press the Home button to display the Lock screen, shown in Figure 1.2. (The iPhone displays this screen for up to about eight seconds, and if you don't do anything, the phone goes into standby mode.) Use your finger to drag the slider all the way to the right. This unlocks the iPhone and then displays the Home screen.

If your iPhone is already on, press the Home button to return to the Home screen. Whatever screen you're currently using will slide away, and the Home screen will take its place.

The Home button also serves two other purposes you should know about:

- If the Home screen is currently displayed, press the Home button to display the Search screen.

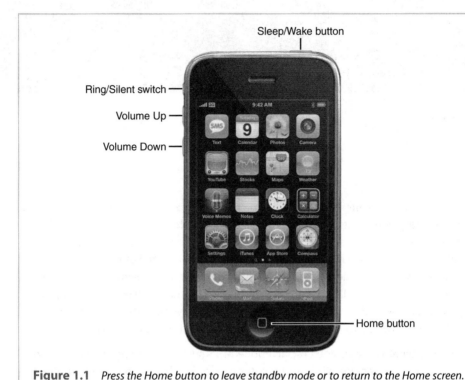

Sleep/Wake button

Ring/Silent switch —

Volume Up —

Volume Down —

Home button

Figure 1.1   *Press the Home button to leave standby mode or to return to the Home screen.*

For the details on searching iPhone data, **see** *"Searching the iPhone," p. 21.*

- If you have an iPhone 4 or iPhone 3GS, press the Home button twice in succession to display a list of your running apps. If you have an older iPhone, press the Home button twice to display a list of your favorite contacts.

Working with the Sleep/Wake Button

If your iPhone is on and you're not using it, the phone will automatically go into standby mode after two minutes. This is called Auto-Lock, and it's a handy feature because it saves battery power when your iPhone is just sitting there. However, you can also put your iPhone into standby mode at any time by using the Sleep/Wake button. You can find this button at the top of your phone. It's the button on the right (pointed out in Figure 1.1, but see Figure 1.5 for a better look), and this button actually has three main functions: sleeping and waking, powering on and off, and handling incoming calls. The next couple of sections cover the first two functions; you learn how to handle incoming calls in Chapter 3, "Placing and Receiving Phone Calls."

Figure 1.2   *On the Lock screen, use your finger to slide the arrow across to unlock your iPhone.*

To learn how to use the Sleep/Wake button to handle incoming phone calls, **see** "Receiving Calls," p. 42.

Sleeping and Waking the iPhone

If you're currently using your iPhone, you can put the phone in standby mode by pressing the Sleep/Week button once. Doing this drops the power consumption considerably. You can still receive incoming calls and texts, but the screen powers down. Tap the Sleep/Wake button again to wake your iPhone. This is just like pressing the Home button: You're prompted with the "slide to unlock" screen, and you drag the slider with your finger to unlock the phone.

Press the Sleep/Wake button to put your phone in standby whenever you're not using the screen. This not only conserves battery power, but it also prevents accidental screen taps. If you have a program such as the iPod running, it will continue to run even after the phone is in standby.

Powering the iPhone On and Off

You can also use the Sleep/Wake button to turn off your iPhone so that it uses no power. This is a good idea if your battery is getting low and you don't think you'll be able to charge it any time soon. You can still periodically check your messages or make an outgoing call when needed, but as long as you turn the phone off when you're done, you minimize the chance that your battery will drain completely. You might also want to turn off your iPhone if you won't be using it for a few days or to solve a problem you are currently having with your phone. (Sometimes turning your iPhone off and then on again can fix a problem.)

 TELL ME MORE   Media 1.1—Understanding the Difference Between Sleep Mode and Power Off Mode

To listen to a free audio recording about the difference between sleep mode and power off mode, log on to my.safaribooksonline.com/9780132182805/media.

To turn off your iPhone, press and hold the Sleep/Wake button for about three seconds, until you see the "slide to power off" control on the screen, as shown in Figure 1.3. Use your finger to drag the slider all the way to the right. The phone shuts down.

Figure 1.3   *Hold down the Sleep/Wake button for a few seconds to see the "slide to power off" screen.*

If you change your mind and decide to leave your iPhone on, tap the Cancel button on the touchscreen. (The "slide to power off" screen will automatically cancel itself if you do nothing for 30 seconds.)

When you're ready to use your iPhone, press and hold the Sleep/Wake button until you see the Apple icon. The iPhone powers up and then displays the Home screen.

When your iPhone is in standby mode, it still communicates with the nearest cell or wireless network to check for new messages. This isn't a problem at home, but it can lead to massive roaming charges if you're overseas. When you travel, always power off your iPhone when you're not using it.

Working with the Ring/Silent Switch

As you will learn in Chapter 3, when a call comes in and you press the Sleep/Wake button once, your iPhone silences the ringer. That's great if you're in a meeting or a movie, but the only problem is that it may take you one or two rings before you can tap Sleep/Wake, and by that time the folks nearby will already be glaring at you.

To prevent this from happening, you can switch your iPhone into silent mode, which means it doesn't ring and it doesn't play any alerts or sound effects. When the sound is turned off, only alarms that you've set using the Clock app will sound. The phone will still vibrate unless you also turn off this feature.

 To learn how to turn off the vibrate feature, **see** "Customizing the iPhone's Sounds," p. 210.

You switch the iPhone between ring and silent modes using the Ring/Silent switch, which is located on the left side of the iPhone, near the top, as shown earlier in Figure 1.1.

Use the following techniques to switch between silent and ring modes:

- To put the phone in silent mode, flick the Ring/Silent switch toward the back of the phone. You see a little orange dot on the switch, the iPhone screen displays a bell with a slash through it, and the phone vibrates briefly. Your iPhone is now in silent mode.

- To resume the normal ring mode, flick the Ring/Silent switch toward the front of the phone. You should not see a little orange dot on the switch, and the iPhone will display a bell on the screen. Your iPhone is now in normal ring mode.

Operating the Volume Controls

The volume controls are on the left side of the iPhone, right below the Ring/Silent switch (refer to Figure 1.1). The button closer to the top of the iPhone is Volume Up, and you press it to increase the volume; the button closer to the bottom of the iPhone is Volume Down, and you press it to decrease the volume. As you adjust the volume, a Speaker icon appears briefly onscreen with filled-in dashes representing the volume level.

You use these buttons to control the volume throughout your iPhone:

- If you're on a call, the volume controls adjust your speaker volume.

- If you're using the iPod application, the volume controls adjust the music volume.

- In all other situations, the volume controls adjust the output of sounds such as alerts and effects.

Getting to Know the Rest of the iPhone

Except for the touchscreen, you need to be familiar with six other physical features of your iPhone.

For starters, the iPhone's bottom panel has three features (see Figure 1.4):

- **Dock connector:** This feature is on the bottom panel of the phone, in the middle of the panel. This is where you connect the cord to either charge your iPhone or hook it up to a computer.

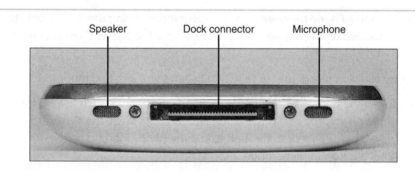

Speaker   Dock connector   Microphone

Figure 1.4 *The iPhone's bottom panel houses the dock connector, speaker, and microphone.*

- **Speaker:** This is located on the bottom panel of your phone, to the left of the dock connector. This is where the sound is broadcast when you turn on the speakerphone or listen to music.

Because the speaker is at the bottom of the phone, you might have trouble hearing it. In that case, turn the iPhone so that the bottom panel is facing you, which should give you better sound quality.

- **Microphone:** This feature is also located on the bottom panel of your phone, to the right of the dock connector panel. This is where the iPhone picks up your voice for phone conversations, recording voicemail, and anything else that requires you to speak.

The iPhone's top and right side panels are home to the Sleep/Wake button and two other features (see Figure 1.5):

- **Headset jack:** The headset jack is located on the top panel of the iPhone. This is where you plug in your headset to listen to music or a phone call.

- **SIM card tray:** You can find this on the right side panel of the iPhone 4 (on earlier models, it's centered on the top panel of the iPhone). To open the tray, gently push the SIM card removal tool (which came with your iPhone; however, a paperclip will also do in a pinch) into the hole on the cover, and then pull the tool toward you. As you pull, the tray comes out. This comes in handy if you want to use another SIM card in your iPhone, or if you need to send your iPhone in for repairs.

The iPhone also comes with a rear-mounted camera lens, as shown in Figure 1.6. When you're using the Camera application, this is what you aim at your subject.

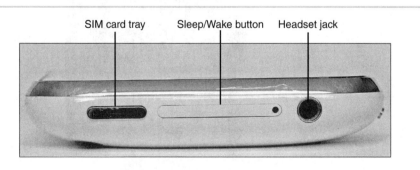

SIM card tray   Sleep/Wake button   Headset jack

Figure 1.5 *The iPhone's top panel holds the Sleep/Wake button as well as the headset jack and the SIM card tray.*

Figure 1.6 *The main camera lens is on the back of the iPhone.*

 To learn more about taking photos with your iPhone, **see** "Taking Photos with the Camera," p. 162.

If you have an iPhone 4, you also get a front-mounted camera, as shown in Figure 1.7. This is great for video chats and taking self-portraits.

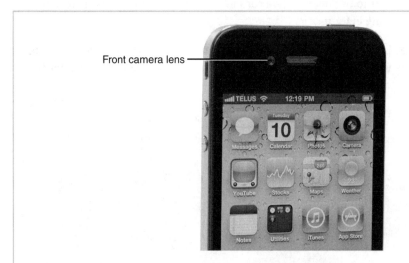

Figure 1.7 *The iPhone 4 also comes with a video chat camera lens on the front.*

Connecting Your iPhone to Your Computer

For the most part, your iPhone lives an independent life and requires no other peripherals or accessories to make it work. However, you might on occasion need to interrupt your iPhone's blissful freedom by connecting it to your Mac or PC. Why would you ever need to do that? There are two main reasons:

- **Charging:** As you see in the next section, your iPhone can charge its battery when it's connected to a computer.

- **Synchronizing:** As you see in Chapter 2, "Learning iPhone Basics," your iPhone needs to be connected to your computer to transfer information.

 To learn more about synchronizing your iPhone and your Mac or PC, **see** *"Synchronizing Your iPhone and Your Computer," p. 30.*

The simplest way to connect your iPhone to your computer is to use the USB cable that came in your iPhone box. Insert the USB connector in a free USB port on your Mac or Windows PC, and then attach the dock connector to the iPhone, as shown in Figure 1.8.

Figure 1.8   *Using your iPhone's USB cable, connect the USB end to your computer, and the dock connector end to the iPhone, as shown here.*

Apple (as well as many third-party vendors) offers an optional iPhone dock, which you can also use to connect your iPhone to your computer. First, you plug the dock into a power outlet. Then, using your iPhone's USB cable, attach the USB end to a free USB port on your Mac or Windows PC and attach the dock connector to the dock. Now insert your iPhone into the dock's cradle as shown in Figure 1.9.

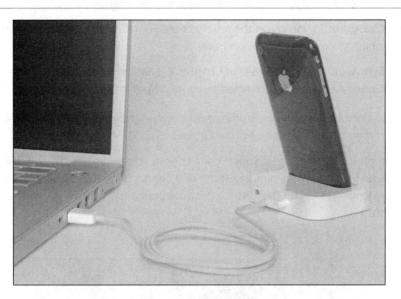

Figure 1.9   *Carefully connect the dock to your computer (as well as to a power outlet), and then insert the iPhone into the dock's cradle.*

By not being careful when using various docking stations available for your iPhone, you could crack or break the dock connector on the bottom of the iPhone.

Charging Your iPhone

You can charge your iPhone by using the cable and adapter that came in the iPhone box. You have a couple of ways to do this:

- Plug the USB end of the cable into the adapter and the other end of the cable into the iPhone's dock connector. Then plug the adapter into an AC outlet and let it charge.

- Plug the USB end of the cable into your computer and the other end of the cable into the iPhone's dock connector. As long as the computer is on and not in sleep mode, it will charge your iPhone.

When the phone is charging, it displays a lightning bolt over the Battery icon unless the screen is locked. If the screen is locked, a large battery gauge indicates that the phone is charging and how full the battery is.

You can also charge your iPhone using a separate docking station, such as the Universal Dock sold by Apple ($49). Just insert your iPhone into the dock, and then connect the dock either to an AC outlet or a computer's USB port.

The iPhone has a built-in battery that is, in Apple parlance, "non-user-serviceable." In English, this just means that you can't remove the battery yourself. Should the battery need replacing, you'll have to send it in to Apple.

In this chapter, you learn a few fundamental
iPhone techniques, including operating the touchscreen and connecting to a network.

2

Learning iPhone Basics

Although your iPhone is flexible and versatile, you'll find that you will use many of
the same operations over and over again. Some of these operations will include
navigation, copy and pasting text, and searches. In this chapter, you learn to perform all of these tasks and more.

None of these tasks are particularly useful unless you have information to work
with, whether the information resides on the Internet or on your main computer.
With that in mind, this chapter also shows you how to connect to a network to give
your iPhone access to the World Wide Web and how to synchronize it to your computer, so that you can access your music, photos, videos, and contacts.

Operating the Touchscreen

The glass front of the iPhone is called the *touchscreen*, and it's arguably the phone's
best feature. You can use the touchscreen to zoom in and out, scroll through lists,
drag items here and there, and even type messages (see Figure 2.1). Amazingly,
the touchscreen requires no external hardware to do all this. You don't need a
stylus or digital pen, and you don't need to attach anything to the iPhone. Instead,
the touchscreen is activated by your finger (or, for some operations, a couple
of fingers).

Navigating the Touchscreen

Take a few moments to try the following maneuvers listed here to get used to the
iPhone touchscreen:

- **Tap:** With your finger, quickly press and release the screen where desired.
  This will allow you to select just about anything on the iPhone. This opens
  applications, activates options, enters text boxes, and much more.

- **Double-tap:** With your finger, tap the touchscreen quickly twice. In apps
  such as Photos or Safari, this technique zooms in on images or parts of web
  pages. A second double-tap zooms back out.

Figure 2.1   *The iPhone relies almost entirely on the touchscreen.*

- **Slide:** Drag your finger across the screen. Doing so enables you to scroll through lists, drag items to different spots, and unlock the iPhone. I use the terms *slide* and *drag* interchangeable throughout this book.

- **Flick:** This is just an exaggerated slide, and it's often useful for scrolling through a long list. Flick your finger across the screen and the iPhone will start scrolling quickly through the list. The faster the flick, the faster the scroll. Touch the screen to stop the scrolling process.

- **Spread and pinch:** This will allow you to zoom in or out on the screen. "To spread" means to move two fingers apart, and you use it to zoom in; "to pinch" means to move two fingers closer together, and you use it to zoom out. This proves especially useful when viewing web pages because the text is often too small to read. Spread your fingers apart to zoom in on the text and thus make it readable, and pinch your fingers together to return to the full screen for easy scrolling and navigation.

- **Two-finger tap:** This is just the tap maneuver but using two fingers rather than one. The only place this is used is in Google Maps. The two-finger tap causes Google Maps to zoom out.

Typing on the Keyboard

You can type on your iPhone, although don't expect to be typing as easily and quickly as you can on your computer. The onscreen keyboard (refer to Figure 1.8) is a bit too small for rapid and accurate typing, but the iPhone does type better than any other phone out there. It even changes depending on the application you use. For example, the keyboard you use when typing into the address bar in Safari doesn't have a Spacebar. In its place, you'll find a period, a slash (/), and a button that enters .com. Web addresses don't use spaces, so Apple replaced the Spacebar with three things that commonly show up in a web address.

To use the keyboard, tap into an area that requires text input. The keyboard will pop up. Tap the keys that you want to enter. As you touch the keys, a magnified version of the letter will pop up. If you touch the wrong key, slide your finger over to the correct one. The keyboard will not enter a key until your finger comes off the screen.

Working with the Special Keys

The keyboard has a few special keys that enable you to do some tricks:

- **Shift:** This key is the upward-pointing arrow to the left of the Z key. Tap this once to engage Shift. The key will glow white, and the next letter you type will be a capital letter. The Shift key then returns to normal automatically. See also the "Activating and Using Caps Lock" section, next.

- **123:** Tap this key to display the numeric keyboard, which includes numbers and most punctuation marks. (Depending on which app you're using, the 123 key will actually display extra characters, such as .?123 or @123.) After you tap it, this key changes to ABC, and you tap ABC to return to the standard keyboard.

- **# + =:** This key appears within the numeric keyboard, and you tap it to display yet another keyboard that contains more punctuation marks as well as a few symbols that aren't used very frequently.

- **Tap-and-hold keys:** Several keys also hide other keys, and you can display these hidden keys by tapping and holding the main key. For example, if you tap and hold the dash (-) key, two extra keys pop up: an em dash (—) and a bullet (•). Similarly, tapping and holding the double quotation (") key displays several types of quotation marks.

- **Backspace:** This key is shaped like a backward arrow with an X inside of it, and you use it to delete characters. Three deletion speeds are available. The first speed deletes in response to a single tap, and it deletes just a single letter; the second speed deletes in response to being held, and it then moves backward through letters and won't stop after a single letter; the third speed kicks in if you hold the delete key long enough, and you use it to delete entire words.

- **Return:** This key works just like the Return or Enter key on a regular keyboard. That is, you use it to start a new paragraph or to select the default option in a screen (for example, the Search button in a Web Search page).

Typing a number or punctuation mark normally requires three taps: tapping 123, tapping the number, and then tapping ABC. Here's a faster way: press and hold the 123 key to open the numeric keyboard, slide the same finger to the number or punctuation you want, and then release the key. This types the number or symbol and returns to the regular keyboard all in one touch.

LET ME TRY IT

Activating and Using Caps Lock

In case you're wondering, the iPhone does offer a Caps Lock feature, but you need to activate it because it's turned off by default. Here are the steps to follow:

1. On the Home screen, tap Settings. The Settings app appears.

2. Tap General. The General screen appears.

3. Tap Keyboard to open the Keyboard screen.

4. Tap the Enable Caps Lock switch to On. The iPhone enables the Caps Lock feature.

5. To switch to Caps Lock while using the keyboard, double-tap the Shift key. The key displays a blue background, which tells you that Caps Lock is on.

LET ME TRY IT

Editing Text

In the previous section I mentioned that you use the Backspace key to delete text, but how do you get the cursor in position for the deletion? Similarly, if you want to insert new text within existing text, how do you position the cursor? For both scenarios, you use the touchscreen, as shown in the following steps:

1. Press and hold your finger on the line you want to edit. The iPhone displays the text inside a magnifying glass, and within that text you see the cursor.

2. While you are holding your finger on the line you want to edit, slide your finger along the line. As you slide, the cursor moves through the text in the same direction.

3.   When the cursor reaches the position where you want make your edits, remove your finger.

Using the Suggestion Feature

If you mistype a word, the iPhone will provide a suggestion in a little bubble underneath the misspelled word. To accept the suggestion, tap the space key or any punctuation key. To ignore the suggestion, tap the suggested word bubble on the screen. This helps save time when you use apostrophes. Leave the apostrophe out and the iPhone will recommend the correct word. For example, if you type **ill**, the iPhone will suggest *I'll*. If *I'll* is the word you want, tap a space or punctuation key to accept the suggestion; if you actually want the word *ill*, instead, tap the suggestion bubble to dismiss the suggestion and leave the text as is.

The Suggestion feature will also show up with unfinished words. The iPhone will guess how you want to finish the word you are typing and provide a suggestion. If the suggestion is the word you want, accept it.

Navigating the Home Screen

When you're using your iPhone, you'll occasionally have to respond to some outside influence, such as answering an incoming phone call or viewing a received text message. However, the majority of what you do with your iPhone will be actions that you initiate yourself. Usually it will include launching an app, so one of the most basic and useful iPhone tasks is navigating the Home screen. Or, I should say, the Home *screens*, because your iPhone can have two or more screens of apps. (In its out-of-the-box configuration, your iPhone actually has three Home screens.)

Navigating multiple Home screens is a good chance to practice your flicking gesture because that's mostly what it's all about:

- Flick to the left to access the next Home screen (that is, the one to the right of the current screen).
- Flick to the right to access the previous Home screen (that is, the one to the left of the current screen).
- Press the Home button to return to the main Home screen from any other screen.

Searching the iPhone

Your iPhone may not have a lot of information on it yet, but later in this chapter you will learn how to synchronize data from your computer to your iPhone. This information can include not only music, photos, and videos, but also contacts, calendars, bookmarks, email accounts, and more. In other words, your iPhone collection of information may be relatively meager at the moment, but it certainly won't stay that way.

Having all that information at your fingertips (literally!) is convenient, for sure, but the more information you have, the more you'll stumble upon an all-too-common problem: *finding* what you need among hundreds, or more likely even *thousands*, of items.

Fortunately, you don't have to waste precious time scouring your iPhone for the information you need. Instead, you can take advantage of the iPhone's search features. There are, in fact, two search features:

- **App searching:** Many apps come with their own search command, which almost always takes the form of a Search box, which you use to type your search text. For example, Figure 2.2 shows the Mail app, which includes a Search box near the top, as well as From, To, Subject, and All buttons that enable you to target your searches.

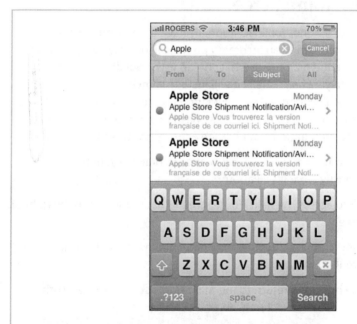

Figure 2.2 *Many apps have their own search features, including the Mail app shown here.*

- **Spotlight:** This feature enables you to search your entire iPhone, which is handy if you're not exactly sure where the data you need can be found.

Before running a Spotlight search, consider customizing the results to show only the data types you really need. On the main Home screen, tap Settings, tap General, tap Home Button, and then tap Search Results. For each type of data you *don't* want in the results, tap it to remove the check mark.

 **LET ME TRY IT**

Running a Spotlight Search

Here are the steps to follow to use Spotlight to search your iPhone:

1. Press the Home button to display the Home screen.

2. Flick right (or press the Home button again). Your iPhone displays the Spotlight screen.

3. Use the Search iPhone box to type your search text. Spotlight displays a list of apps, messages, contacts, bookmarks, and so on that match your search text, as shown in Figure 2.3.

Figure 2.3 *Use the Spotlight screen to search for data throughout your iPhone.*

If you see the item you want, tap it in the results list to open the item.

Cutting, Copying, and Pasting Data

Your iPhone is an amazingly useful device even if you only use it to view and read information. However, your iPhone becomes a real productivity booster when you also use it to *work with* information. By "working with" information, I'm talking about selecting text or images, copying (or, in the case of some text, cutting) information, and then pasting it elsewhere.

You probably know how useful this is on a computer, but you might be wondering just how often you'd need to do any of this on an iPhone. Actually, once you know how it works, chances are you'll find yourself copying and pasting data all the time. For example, you might need to copy a website address to use in a text message, you might need to select some web page text for use in an email message, or you might want to copy an image from an email message or a website to use as your iPhone wallpaper.

Whatever your reason, you need to know how to select, copy (or cut), and then paste it in your iPhone.

 LET ME TRY IT

Selecting Text

1. Open the document that contains the text you want to select.

2. Display the text onscreen and zoom in so that you can see the text more clearly, while still keeping the entire text passage in view (if possible).

3. Make the initial text selection. How you do this depends on whether the text is editable (such as text in an email message) or noneditable (such as text in a web page):

   - **Editable text:** Tap and hold on the first word of the text, and then tap the Select button.
   - **Non-editable text:** Tap and hold on the first word of the text.
     Your iPhone selects the word and displays selection handles around it, as shown in Figure 2.4. (You can ignore the Copy button for now.) The left handle that appears above the text marks the start point of the selection; the right handle that appears below the text marks the end point of the selection.

4. Drag the endpoint handle to the right and down. As you drag the endpoint, your iPhone selects more text.

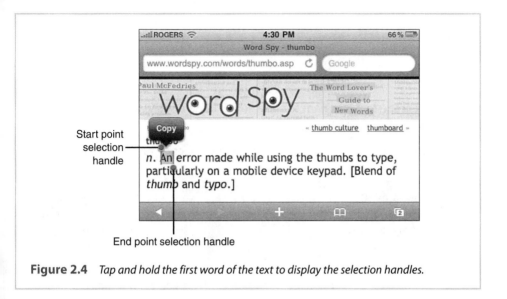

Start point
selection
handle

End point selection handle

Figure 2.4 *Tap and hold the first word of the text to display the selection handles.*

5. When all the text you want is selected, release the endpoint handle. Your iPhone selects the text, as shown in Figure 2.5.

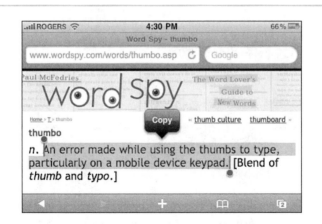

Figure 2.5 *Drag the endpoint selection handle down and to the right until all your text is selected.*

SHOW ME Media 2.1—A Video About Copying and Pasting Text on Your iPhone

Access this video file through your registered Web Edition at my.safaribooksonline.com/9780132182805/media.

 **LET ME TRY IT**

Copying and Pasting Text

1. Select the text you want to copy. Your iPhone displays a Copy button above the selected text (see Figure 2.5).

2. Tap Copy. Your iPhone loads a copy of the selected text into memory.

> If the text is editable, you will see *two* buttons above your selection: Copy and Cut. If you need to move the text to another location, tap the Cut button rather than the Copy button.

3. If necessary, open the document or app where you want to paste the text.

4. Position the cursor where you want the text to appear.

5. Tap the cursor. Your iPhone displays the buttons shown in Figure 2.6.

Figure 2.6   *Tap the cursor and then tap Paste to paste your copied text.*

6. Tap Paste. Your iPhone pastes the text.

 **LET ME TRY IT**

Copying and Pasting an Image

1. Tap and hold the image you want to copy. Your iPhone displays the options shown in Figure 2.7.

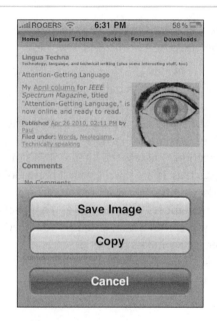

Figure 2.7   *Tap and hold an image to see these options.*

2. Tap Copy. Your iPhone stores a copy of the image in memory.

3. Open the document or app where you want to paste the image.

4. Position the cursor where you want the image to appear.

5. Tap the cursor.

6. Tap Paste. Your iPhone pastes the image.

Undoing a Paste

If you paste an image in the wrong place, or if you paste the wrong text, you don't have to delete the pasted data by hand. To reverse your most recent paste, give your iPhone a sharp shake and then tap the Undo Paste command that appears.

Connecting to a Wireless Network

If you have a data plan with your cellular provider, you can use your iPhone to access email, the Web, and other online services in any location that has a cellular signal. Ideally you want a nice, fast 3G signal, but your iPhone can also work with slower EDGE signals in a pinch.

TELL ME MORE   Media 2.2—Understanding Cellular and Wireless Networks

To listen to a free audio recording about cellular and wireless networks, log on to my.safaribooksonline.com/9780132182805/media.

However, data plans often come with bandwidth limits, so your iPhone assumes that if a nearby wireless network offers Internet access and you can connect to that network, you'd rather use a wireless connection than a cellular one. (And, of course, if your cellular plan doesn't come with a data component, you have no choice but to use a wireless connection to access the Internet.) This means that whenever you load an Internet app, such as Safari or Mail, your iPhone looks for nearby wireless networks and then asks whether you want to connect with one of them. If you do connect, your iPhone remembers that network and connects to it automatically in the future the next time it comes within range. So you need to know how to use your iPhone to connect to a wireless network.

LET ME TRY IT

Connecting to a Wireless Network

1. Tap to open the Internet app you want to use, such as Safari or Mail. Your iPhone displays a list of nearby wireless networks, as shown in Figure 2.8.

2. Tap the network you want to use. If the network is secure, your iPhone prompts you to enter the network password.

3. Type the password.

4. Tap Join. Your iPhone connects to the network and replaces the status bar's 3G (or E) icon with the Wireless icon, as shown in Figure 2.9.

Figure 2.8   *Launch an Internet app to see a list of nearby wireless networks.*

Figure 2.9   *When you're connected to a wireless network, the status bar displays the Wireless icon rather than the 3G icon.*

If a network is not secure, only connect to it if you're sure you have permission to use the network. There have been recent cases where people connecting to unsecured networks without permission have been charged with theft of services!

Synchronizing Your iPhone and Your Computer

Synchronizing your iPhone means transferring information between your iPhone and your computer. Two things happen during a sync operation:

- Information gets sent from your computer to your iPhone. This usually involves items stored on your computer such as music, photos, videos, contacts, and appointments.

- Information gets sent from your iPhone to your computer. This usually involves items created on your iPhone, such as photos or videos you've taken with the camera, contacts you've added to the Contacts app, appointments you added to the Calendar app, and so on.

The idea here is that by keeping your iPhone and your computer in sync, you always have all the data you need, whether you're at home, at the office, or on the road. Fortunately, syncing happens automatically when you connect your iPhone to your computer, as described in Chapter 1, "Getting to Know Your iPhone." As soon as your computer detects that your iPhone is connected, it opens the iTunes application and iTunes runs the synchronization.

> ⌘ *To learn how to connect your iPhone to your Mac or Windows PC, **see** "Connecting Your iPhone to Your Computer," p. 13.*

However, by default iTunes includes only a subset of your data during the synchronization. For best syncing, you should tell iTunes exactly what you want synced. Most of the rest of this book's chapters include the details on syncing specific types of data. For example, Chapter 6, "Managing Music on Your iPhone," includes a section on synchronizing music.

> ⌘ *For the detail on syncing music to your iPhone, **see** "Synchronizing Music," p. 95.*

So rather than repeat those details here, I'll just take you through the basic procedure for setting up your iPhone for syncing.

SHOW ME   Media 2.3—A Video About Syncing Your iPhone with Your
Computer
Access this video file through your registered Web edition at
my.safaribooksonline.com/9780132182805/media.

LET ME TRY IT

Configuring Your iPhone for Syncing

1. Connect your iPhone to your Mac or Windows PC. Note that it might take a
   little while for iTunes to load and recognize your iPhone.

2. In the iTunes sidebar, click your iPhone in the Devices branch. iTunes displays the Summary tab, as shown in Figure 2.10.

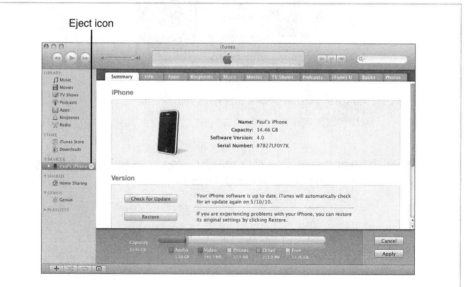

Figure 2.10   *Click your iPhone in the Devices list to see this Summary tab.*

3. Use the other tabs—Info, Apps, Music, and so on—to choose the data you
   want to synchronize. Again, see the relevant chapters throughout this
   book to learn the details about each tab.

4. Click Apply. iTunes synchronizes your iPhone. While the sync is occurring,
   you see the screen shown in Figure 2.11, and you can't use your iPhone

until the sync is complete. (Although you can cancel the sync at any time
by dragging the slider.)

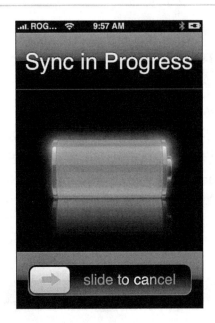

Figure 2.11   *You see this screen while iTunes syncs your iPhone.*

5. When the sync is complete, click the Eject icon (refer to Figure 2.10) next to
    your iPhone's name in the iTunes Devices list.

3

Placing and Receiving Phone Calls

A *Swiss-army phone* is a cell phone that contains multiple tools, and your iPhone certainly qualifies. It's a web browser, an email client, a contacts and schedule manager, a media player, an eBook reader, and on and on. But, first and foremost, your iPhone is a *phone*, so it's important that you get familiar with its phone features. In this chapter, you learn the various ways that your iPhone enables you to place phone calls, including the rather amazing feats of placing phone calls directly from web pages and email messages. You also learn how to receive incoming calls, set up and work with visual voicemail, use a Bluetooth headset, exchange text messages, and more.

Placing Calls

Placing a phone call seems like the simplest and most straightforward of tasks: You tap out the phone number and everything proceeds from there. Your iPhone makes placing phone calls simple, but it also provides you with quite a few features that make it even easier and more convenient to dial calls.

Dialing a Call

If you know the number you want to dial, your iPhone has an onscreen keypad that you can use to tap the number and place the call.

If your cellular plan allows you only so many minutes, you should keep track of your usage to avoid extra charges. Fortunately, you can do this right on your iPhone. On the Home screen, tap Settings, tap General, and then tap Usage. In the Usage screen that appears, locate the Call Time section and read the Current Period value.

 **LET ME TRY IT**

Dialing a Call

1. On the Home screen, tap the Phone icon. Your iPhone launches the Phone app.

2. In the menu bar at the bottom of the screen, tap Keypad. The Phone app displays the keypad.

3. Tap the numbers on the keypad. As you tap, the phone number appears above the keypad, as shown in Figure 3.1. If you make a mistake, tap the Delete key, to the right of the Call button.

Figure 3.1 *In the Phone app's Keypad screen, the numbers you tap appear above the keypad.*

4. Tap Call. Your iPhone dials the number. When the call is connected, you see a screen like the one shown in Figure 3.2.

5. If you need to enter a digit during the call (for example, if you're working with a telephone menu system), tap the Keypad icon, tap the number, and then tap Hide Keypad.

6. If you'd prefer to hear the caller through the iPhone's speaker, tap the Speaker icon.

Figure 3.2   *You see a screen similar to this while you're on the call.*

7.   When your call is done, tap End.

If you have an iPhone 4, when you're on a call your screen will look slightly different than the one shown in Figure 3.2. Instead of the Hold icon, you see an icon called FaceTime. If the person you're talking to is also using an iPhone 4 and both of you are connected to a wireless network, then you can tap FaceTime to initiate a video call.

Redialing a Recent Call

One of the iPhone's key features is that it gives you multiple ways to dial calls quickly and efficiently. A great example of this is when you need to redial a call you recently placed. In the worst-case scenario, you might not remember the number, and so you have to look it up all over again. Even if you remember the number, you still have to redial it, which can take time and isn't guaranteed to be problem free. (You might dial the wrong number, for example.)

Fortunately, the Phone app comes with a Recents feature that remembers the calls you placed and enables you to redial a call with just a couple of taps.

LET ME TRY IT

Redialing a Recent Call

1. On the Home screen, tap the Phone icon. Your iPhone launches the Phone app.

2. In the menu bar at the bottom of the screen, tap Recents. The Phone app displays your most recent phone calls, as shown in Figure 3.3.

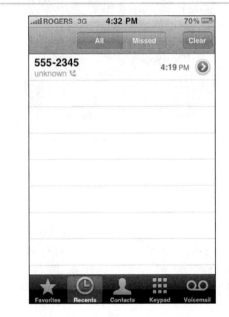

Figure 3.3 *Use the Phone app's Recents screen to quickly redial a recent phone number.*

3. Tap the number you want to redial. The Phone app automatically redials the number for you.

4. When your call is done, tap End.

Dialing a Contact

In Chapter 7, "Managing Contacts on Your iPhone," you learn how to sync, add, and edit contacts using your iPhone's Contacts app. In particular, you learn how to add one or more phone numbers for a contact. After you've done that, you can use your iPhone's Contacts list to quickly dial that person.

*To learn how to assign phone numbers to your contacts, **see** "Adding a Phone Number to a Contact," p. 116.*

LET ME TRY IT

Dialing a Contact

1. On the Home screen, tap the Phone icon to open the Phone app.

2. In the menu bar at the bottom of the screen, tap Contacts. The Phone app displays your Contacts list.

> You can also display your Contacts list using the Contacts app. From the Home screen, tap the Contacts icon.

3. Scroll through the contacts until you find the one you want to call.

4. Tap the contact. Your iPhone displays the contact's data, as shown in Figure 3.4.

5. Tap the phone number you want to use to call the contact. The Phone app dials the number for you.

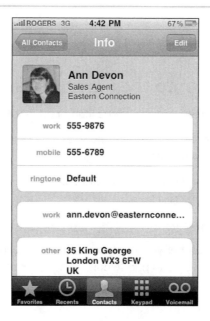

Figure 3.4   *Tap the contact you want to call; then tap the phone number.*

6. When your call is done, tap End.

Dialing via the Favorites List

You probably have a few numbers that you call frequently. It could be your home number, your spouse's cell number, or your local pizza place. The more you call a particular number, the more time you'll save if you can figure out some way to place those calls quickly. You might think the Recents list, described earlier, is the way to go here, and that will certainly work most of the time. However, the Recents list will eventually get crowded with other numbers, so it's not the most efficient way to call frequent numbers. Similarly, the Contacts list isn't the best way, either, because you have to scroll through your contacts to find the person you want to call.

The most efficient way to dial frequently called numbers is to use the Phone app's Favorites list, which places any number just a couple of taps away.

SHOW ME   Media 3.1—A Video About Adding Phone Numbers to the iPhone's Favorites List

Access this video file through your registered Web Edition at my.safaribooksonline.com/9780132182805/media.

LET ME TRY IT

Adding a Number to the Favorites List

1. On the Home screen, tap the Phone icon to open the Phone app.

2. In the menu bar at the bottom of the screen, tap Favorites. The Phone app displays your Favorites list.

3. Tap the Add icon (+) in the upper-right corner of the screen. Your iPhone opens the All Contacts screen.

4. Tap the contact you want to add as a favorite.

5. Tap the phone number you want to call from the Favorites list. The Phone app adds the contact and phone number to the Favorites list.

 **LET ME TRY IT**

Dialing via the Favorites List

1. On the Home screen, tap the Phone icon to open the Phone app.

2. In the menu bar at the bottom of the screen, tap Favorites. The Phone app displays your Favorites list, as shown in Figure 3.5.

3. Tap the favorite you want to call. The Phone app dials the number for you.

4. When your call is completed, tap End.

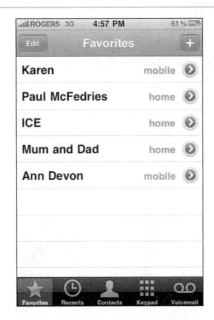

Figure 3.5 *In the Favorites list, tap the number you want to call.*

Dialing a Call from a Web Page

One of your iPhone's most surprising—and most useful—features is its capability to not only recognize phone numbers embedded in web pages, but also to let you dial any one of those numbers with just a couple of taps. This might seem of limited usefulness, but you'd be surprised how many web pages have phone numbers in them. For example, how often have you searched a company's website looking for a customer service or technical support phone number? If you do your searching on your iPhone, you can call any number you find without having to memorize or write down the number.

 **LET ME TRY IT**

Dialing a Call from a Web Page

1. Use your iPhone's Safari web browser to open the page that contains the phone number.

2. Scroll the phone number into view.

3. If necessary, spread your fingers over the phone number to magnify the page and get a good look at the number.

4. Tap the phone number. Your iPhone prompts you to call the number, as shown in Figure 3.6.

5. Tap Call. Your iPhone dials the number.

6. When your call is completed, tap End.

Figure 3.6 *Tap a phone number on a web page, and your iPhone offers to dial the number for you.*

Dialing a Call from an Email Message

Lots of people include phone numbers in email messages. For example, many people sign their messages with contact data, including one or more phone numbers. Similarly, an information message from a company or person might include a phone number you can call for more data. Instead of dialing that number by memorizing it, writing it down on a piece of paper, or even using your iPhone copy-and-paste features, you can dial the number directly from the email message.

 **LET ME TRY IT**

Dialing a Call from an Email Message

1. Use your iPhone's Mail app to open the message that contains the phone number.

2. Scroll the phone number into view.

3. Tap the phone number. Your iPhone prompts you to call the number, as shown in Figure 3.7.

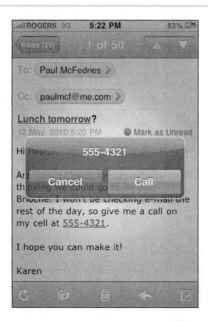

Figure 3.7   *Tap a phone number in an email message to get your iPhone to dial the number.*

4. Tap Call. Your iPhone dials the number.

5. When your call is done, tap End.

Using Your Voice to Dial a Call

The dialing methods you've seen so far are all handy in different ways, but they're also "handy" in the sense that you must have at least one hand free for tapping. What do you do if you've got both hands on your hamburger or are unprepared to tap? In such situations, you can take advantage of the Voice Control feature found on the iPhone 4 and the iPhone 3GS, which lets you make voice-dial calls.

 **LET ME TRY IT**

Using Your Voice to Dial a Call

1. Tap and hold the Home button. If you have Apple's iPhone headset, you can also press and hold the center button. Your iPhone displays the Voice Control screen.

2. Say "call" or "phone."

3. If the person you want to call is in your Contacts list, say the person's name and then say the label of the phone number (such as "work" or "mobile"; if you're not sure of the label, you can skip that part). For anyone else, say the phone number you want to call.

4. If you specified a contact who has multiple numbers and you didn't say a label, you'll see the Multiple Numbers version of the Voice Control screen, shown in Figure 3.8; you now need to say the label of the number you want to dial. Your iPhone dials the number.

5. When your call is done, tap End.

Receiving Calls

Like placing outgoing phone calls, answering incoming phone calls seems like a straightforward bit of business: The calls comes in, you answer it. That's true enough, as far as it goes, but you should be starting to learn that the iPhone always has a few extra tricks up its digital sleeve. In this case, the iPhone offers several other call-receiving features, including letting you send a call directly to voicemail, putting a caller on hold, and even setting up conference calls.

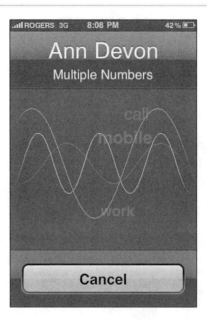

Figure 3.8   *If a contact has two or more phone numbers, use the Multiple Numbers screen to say the label of the number you want to dial.*

Answering a Call

When a call comes in, your iPhone checks the caller's phone number to see whether it matches anyone in your iPhone's Contacts list. If the number doesn't match, you see Unknown at the top of the screen; if it does match, you see the contact's name at the top of the screen, as well as the label associated with the number (such as work or mobile). If you've added a photo for that person, you see that person's photo in the background, as shown in Figure 3.9. Tap the Answer button to answer the call and begin your conversation.

If you have an iPhone 4 and you're currently connected to a wireless network, the incoming call might say *Contact* would like FaceTime (where *Contact* is the person's name). This means the caller wants to initiate a FaceTime video call with you. In this case, tap Accept to start the video call, or tap Decline the video call.

Figure 3.9 *If your iPhone recognizes the number of the incoming call, it displays the person's name, the label associated with the number, and the person's photo.*

Declining a Call

When a call comes in, you might not be in a position to answer, or you might not feel like talking to whomever's calling. Normally, your iPhone rings four times before it automatically sends the caller to your voicemail system. If you don't feel like waiting for all four rings, particularly if you think the ringing might disturb the people nearby, you have two choices:

- Tap the Decline button that appears when your iPhone detects an incoming call (refer to Figure 3.9).
- Press the Sleep/Wake button twice.

Either way, your iPhone sends the call directly to voicemail, which is useful in situations where you don't want the ringing to disturb your neighbors and you don't want to answer the call. Note that, in this case, you don't have the option of answering the call.

Silencing a Call

The problem with declining a call, as described in the previous section, is you're giving yourself away to a certain extent by sending the call to voicemail before the usual four rings. If savvy callers hear only one or two rings before voicemail kicks in, they will know you're screening your calls.

If you prefer to give a caller the standard four rings, but you don't want the ringing to bother your neighbors, you can turn off the ringer. To silence an incoming call, press the Sleep/Wake button once. This temporarily turns off the ringer, but you still have the standard four "rings" to answer, should you decide to. If you don't answer, your iPhone sends the call to your voicemail.

Putting a Caller on Hold to Answer Another Call

When you're on a call using a regular phone and another call comes in, you have three ways to handle the new call: You can ignore it, you can put your current caller on hold and answer the incoming call, or you can end your current call and then answer the new call.

Amazingly, you get the same three options with your iPhone. If you're mid-conversation with a caller and a new call comes in, your iPhone displays the name, number label, and picture of the new caller (if that data is stored in your iPhone, that is), and you see three buttons, as shown in Figure 3.10:

- **Ignore:** Tap this button to redirect the incoming call to your voicemail.

- **Hold Call + Answer:** Tap this button to put your current caller on hold and answer the incoming call.

- **End Call + Answer:** Tap this button to disconnect the current caller and answer the incoming call.

 **LET ME TRY IT**

Putting a Caller on Hold to Answer an Incoming Call

1. When the new call comes in, tap Hold Call + Answer. Your iPhone displays a screen similar to the one shown in Figure 3.11, which shows your callers, particularly your original caller at the top with a status of HOLD.

2. To switch from one caller to another, tap the Swap icon.

3. To end one of the calls, tap the caller and then tap End Call.

Figure 3.10   *You see this screen if another calls comes in while you're using the phone.*

Figure 3.11   *You see this screen when you have a caller on hold.*

Setting Up a Conference Call

In the previous section, you learned that you can use your iPhone to juggle two calls by placing one call on hold and then swapping the two callers as needed. That's a great way to go if you want to keep each call private, but there are plenty of situations where swapping callers is inconvenient and it would be better just to talk to everyone simultaneously. This is known as a *conference call*, and it's useful whether you're trying to plan a business strategy with several colleagues or a night out on the town with several friends. Your iPhone has all the tools you need to set up a conference call.

 SHOW ME   Media 3.2—A Video About Setting Up a Conference Call on Your iPhone
Access this video file through your registered Web Edition at my.safaribooksonline.com/9780132182805/media.

 LET ME TRY IT

Setting Up a Conference Call

1. Place the initial phone call.

If you're already talking to two people, with one person on hold, you can convert these separate calls into a conference call by tapping the merge calls icon.

2. Tap the Add Call icon.

3. Place the next call. Note that you can use any method: the keypad, contacts, favorites, recents, and so on. When the next call goes through, your iPhone puts the initial caller on hold.

4. Tap the Merge Calls icon. Your iPhone merges the calls into a conference call and displays Conference at the top of the call screen (as well as a scrolling list of the caller names), as shown in Figure 3.12.

5. Repeat steps 2 to 4 to add more people to the conference call.

6. To display a list of the callers, tap the Info icon (pointed out in Figure 3.12).

Figure 3.12   *With your conference call on the go, you see this call screen.*

Your iPhone displays a screen like the one shown in Figure 3.13.

7. To speak with a caller privately, tap the Private button next to that person's

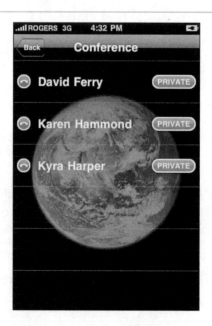

Figure 3.13   *Tap the Info icon to see a list of your callers.*

name or number. Your iPhone places the other callers on hold. When you're done, tap the Merge Calls icon to return to the conference call.

8. To drop a caller from the conference call, tap the red Phone icon to the left of the person's name or number and then tap End Call.

9. To add an incoming caller to the conference call, tap Hold Call + Answer and then, once you're connected, tap the Merge Calls icon.

10. To end the conference call, tap Back to return to the call screen and then tap End Call.

Working with Visual Voicemail

With most voicemail features, you need to call up a remote system, jump through a hoop or two to get to your mailbox, and then listen to your messages sequentially. Your iPhone does away with all that. If you've signed up for the Visual Voicemail feature with your cellular provider, your iPhone stores your messages right on the phone. This means you always have access to your messages. The iPhone's interface makes it easy to hear and work with messages, and you can listen to your messages in any order you want.

Recording Your Visual Voicemail Greeting

The first thing you need to do is record the greeting message that incoming callers hear if you choose not to (or simply can't) answer your phone or if you decline the call, as described earlier.

 **LET ME TRY IT**

Recording Your Visual Voicemail Greeting

1. In the Phone app, tap Voicemail in the menu bar to open the Voicemail screen. If this is the first time you've tapped Voicemail, the Phone app will ask you to enter a numeric password (which allows you to retrieve your messages from another phone). It will then display the Greeting screen, so you can skip step 2.

2. Tap Greeting to open the Greeting screen, shown in Figure 3.14.

3. Tap Custom.

Figure 3.14   *Use the Greeting screen to record your Visual Voicemail greeting.*

4. Tap Record.

5. Speak clearly into the iPhone to record your message.

6. When you've finished your message, tap Stop.

7. To review the greeting, tap Play.

8. If you're not satisfied with the message, repeat steps 4 to 7.

9. When your message is just right, tap Save.

Listening to Visual Voicemail Messages

Your iPhone gives you several indications that you have one or more voicemail messages waiting for you:

- If your iPhone is in sleep mode, a message pops up telling you that a voice-mail message was left, as well as the name or number of the caller.

- On the Home screen, the Phone app's icon displays a red badge in the upper-right corner that tells you how many voicemail messages you have waiting. (Note, however, that this number also includes any recent calls that you missed.)

- In the Phone app, the Voicemail icon displays a badge in the upper-right corner that tells you how many unheard voicemail messages you have.

To see your messages, tap the Voicemail icon to open the Voicemail screen, shown in Figure 3.15. This screen displays a list of your messages, and for each message you see a blue dot if the message is unheard, the name of the caller (if that caller is in your Contacts list) or number of the caller (if the caller is unknown), and the time the message was left (if the message came in today) or the date the message was left (if the message came in prior to today).

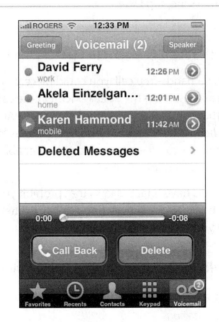

Figure 3.15   *Tap the Phone app's Voicemail icon to see a list of your Visual Voicemail messages.*

 **LET ME TRY IT**

Listening to Visual Voicemail Messages

1. In the Phone app, tap the Voicemail icon in the menu bar to open the Voicemail screen.

2. Tap a message. Your iPhone begins playing the message. If you want to play the message through the iPhone's speaker, tap the Speaker icon.

3. To pause the playback, tap the message; to resume playback, tap the message again; to fast-forward or rewind the message, drag the ball in the playback bar forward or backward.

4. To see more information about the caller, tap the blue "more info" arrow next to the sender's name or number. In the Info screen that appears, you see the time and date that the message arrived, and the sender's contact information if the sender is in your Contacts list.

5. To phone the caller, tap the Call Back button.

6. To remove the message, tap Delete.

Pairing Your iPhone to a Bluetooth Headset

If you need to conduct a hands-free call, you could place your iPhone on a table or other nearby surface and then tap the Speaker icon in the call screen, which lets you hear your caller through the iPhone's built-in speaker. An even better solution is to use a Bluetooth *headset*, which combines headphones for listening and a microphone for talking. *Bluetooth* is a technology that enables you to connect—or *pair*—two devices without the use of wires.

A number of jurisdictions have enacted laws that prohibit you from using your phone while driving, but they are allowing you to use a Bluetooth headset to make hands-free calls from your car.

TELL ME MORE   Media 3.3—Understanding Bluetooth

To listen to a free audio recording about Bluetooth networking, log on to my.safaribooksonline.com/9780132182805/media.

LET ME TRY IT

Pairing Your iPhone to a Bluetooth Headset

1. On the Home screen, tap Settings to open the Settings screen.

2. Tap General to open the General screen.

3. Tap Bluetooth to open the Bluetooth screen.

4. Tap the Bluetooth switch to the On position. Your iPhone immediately begins looking for nearby Bluetooth devices.

5. If the headset has a separate switch or button that makes the device discoverable, turn on that switch or press that button. Wait until you see the correct headset name appear in the Bluetooth screen.

6. Tap the name of the Bluetooth headset. Your iPhone pairs with the headset automatically, and you see Connected next to the device name, as shown in Figure 3.16.

Figure 3.16 *In the Bluetooth screen, make sure the Bluetooth switch is On, make sure your headset is discoverable, and then tap the headset to make the connection.*

In this chapter, you learn how to use your iPhone
to surf websites and work with web pages.

4

Surfing the Web on Your iPhone

Microsoft founder and chairman Bill Gates is famous for many things, including
being the world's richest person (until recently, anyway) and being the world's
unofficial Alpha Geek. However, in tech circles he's also famous for his longstanding
vision for Microsoft and for computing as a whole: Information at Your Fingers. It's
the simple yet transforming idea that, as Gates himself once put it, "Any piece of
information you want should be available to you." The idea wasn't new—the motto
of the Information Industry Association back in the 1970s was "Putting Information
at Your Fingertips"—but Gates championed it as early as 1989, and it remained his
overriding goal for the next two decades.

In fact, you could argue that Information at Your Fingertips has been the goal for
the entire tech sector for the past 20 years, and particularly since the Internet
became mainstream. And a funny thing happened between then and now: Quietly
and without much fuss or fanfare, the seemingly futuristic goal of Information at
Your Fingertips is now pretty much a reality. Paradoxically, that reality exists not so
much because of anything Microsoft did, but because of what Microsoft competi-
tor Apple did: It invented the iPhone and, in particular, it supplied the iPhone with
Safari, an amazing web browser.

Somebody at dinner claims that Dustin Hoffman was in *Star Wars*? Whip out your
iPhone and look it up in the Internet Movie Database (http://www.imdb.com).
Wondering whether that restaurant you see out your car window is any good?
Wake up your iPhone and see what Chowhound (http://chowhound.chow.com) has
to say.

If the idea of having information literally at your fingertips appeals to you, this
chapter shows you how to use your iPhone's Safari web browser to get practically
any information you need, whenever you need it.

Surfing Web Pages

Mobile phones have had web browsers for many years, but they weren't appealing
as web surfing devices because they had tiny screens that displayed either garbled

versions of web pages or stripped-down "mobile" versions of web pages. The iPhone changed all that by offering a relatively large screen, and by offering Safari, a web browser that renders web pages beautifully. The screen is still a bit too small for truly comfortable web surfing, but with the iPhone's built-in zooming and scrolling features, any website can become readable in seconds.

The next few sections take you through some techniques for using your iPhone to navigate web pages. Before moving on, start the Safari web browser by tapping the Safari icon on the iPhone Home screen. Figure 4.1 shows the Safari web browser screen and points out some of its features.

Figure 4.1 *On your iPhone, you use the Safari web browser to surf the Web.*

If your cellular data plan allows you to use only a certain number of megabytes or gigabytes of data, you should monitor your usage to avoid going over. In the Home screen, tap Settings, tap General, tap Usage, and then read the Cellular Network Data values.

Entering a Web Page Address

Perhaps the most straightforward way to navigate to a web page using your iPhone is to enter the page's address in Safari's Address box. Your iPhone helps you out by displaying a version of the onscreen keyboard (see Figure 4.2) that includes special keys designed for web page addresses, including a .com key, a backslash (/) key, and a dot (.) key.

Figure 4.2 *Your iPhone's Safari browser offers special keys that make it easier to enter web page addresses.*

If you tap and hold the .com key, the iPhone pops up four related keys: .net, .edu, .org, and .us, which are commonly used in Web page addresses. Drag your finger to the key you want to use, and then release your finger to select it.

 **LET ME TRY IT**

Entering a Web Page Address

1. Tap inside the Address box. Your iPhone opens the Address box and displays the keyboard.

If you can't see the Address box, perhaps you've scrolled too far down the screen. Tap the iPhone's status bar at the top of the screen to bring the status bar back up.

2. Use the keyboard to tap the address of the page you want to view.

3. Tap Go. Your iPhone displays the web page.

Tapping Links

Another way that you can use your iPhone to surf the Web is to follow the links that appear on the pages you visit. On your iPhone, following a link is a simple as tapping on it. If you'd prefer to know the address of the page before following the link, you can tap and hold the link as described in the following steps.

 **LET ME TRY IT**

Viewing a Link Address

1. Tap and hold the link. Safari displays the options shown in Figure 4.3.

Figure 4.3 *Tap and hold a link to see these options.*

2. Read the link address, which appears just above the Open command.

3. If the address looks okay, tap Open. If the address points to a site you don't want to visit, tap Cancel instead.

Opening a Link in a New Page

When you're viewing a web page, you might want to open a link but also keep your current page open in the browser. Doing so proves useful, for example, if you want to compare the data on the two pages, or if you want to quickly check something on the other page and then return to the current page. Your iPhone's Safari browser accommodates multiple sites simultaneously by enabling you to open multiple browser windows, which Safari calls *pages*. You can open up to eight separate browsing pages.

 LET ME TRY IT

Opening a Link in a New Page

1. Tap and hold the link. Safari displays the options shown earlier in Figure 4.3.

2. Tap Open in New page. Safari creates a new page, loads the linked site into the new page, and then displays the page.

3. To switch pages, first tap the Pages icon in the lower-right corner of the Safari screen (see Figure 4.1, earlier). Safari displays thumbnail versions of the open pages, as shown in Figure 4.4.

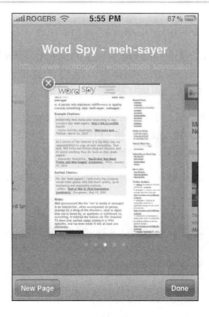

Figure 4.4 *Tap the Pages icon to see thumbnail versions of your open websites.*

4. Scroll left or right until you see the page you want to view.

5. Tap the thumbnail. Safari displays the page.

To close a page, tap the Pages icon, scroll left or right until you bring the page into view, and then tap the red X icon in the upper-left corner of the page thumbnail.

Surfing with the History List

As you surf the Web, your iPhone's Safari browser keeps track of the pages you visit and maintains a list of the pages you've visited recently. This is called the History list because it's a summary of your recent browsing history. If you want to redisplay a site you visited in the past few days and you don't remember the address or how you got there, you will find the site in the History list. Then, you just tap the site in the History list to load the site into Safari.

 **LET ME TRY IT**

Surfing with the History List

1. Tap the Bookmarks icon, shown earlier in Figure 4.1.

2. Tap History. (If you don't see the History item, tap the button in the upper-left corner until you see the History item.) Safari opens the History list, as shown in Figure 4.5.

3. Pages you just visited today are displayed at the top of the list, and if you see the one you want, tap it to load the page into Safari. Otherwise, tap the day on which you visited the page.

4. Tap the page you want to revisit. Safari displays the page.

If other people use your iPhone, you might not want them to see your browsing history. To prevent this, display the History list, tap Clear, and then when Safari asks you to confirm, tap Clear History.

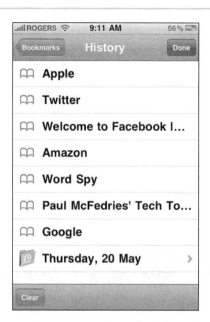

Figure 4.5   *Use Safari's History list to revisit websites you've recently surfed.*

Searching the Web

Having information at your fingertips is easy with your iPhone *if* you know where to find that information. Unfortunately (or, really, *fortunately*), the Web is home to billions upon billions of pages, so although the information you seek is almost certainly out there somewhere, *finding* the information is another matter.

That's where the Web's search engines come in, particularly the Google search engine (http://www.google.com). When you type a word or two or three that identifies the information you seek, the search engine will look for pages that match your terms and then display those sites in a list, ranked with the best matches at the top (just below the Sponsored Links section, which features ads related to your search term).

Even better, your iPhone's Safari browser comes with a Google search feature built in, so you don't have to visit the Google site to perform these searches.

 **LET ME TRY IT**

Searching the Web

1. Tap inside the Search box at the top of the Safari screen. Your iPhone opens the Search box and displays the keyboard.

2. Use the keyboard to tap a word, multiple words, or phrase (enclosed in quotation marks) that you think will represent the information you're looking for.

3. Tap Search. Your iPhone passes along your search text to Google, which then displays the search results.

4. If you see a result that appears to be a good match for the information you seek, tap the page's link in the search results. Your iPhone will display the web page.

Working with Web Pages

Once you've surfed to a web page, you might think all that's left to do is read the text, view its pictures, and then move on to the next page. You can certainly do all that, but the Safari browser offers a number of other features and tools to help you work with a web page once you have it up on the screen. For example, you can scroll and zoom the page for easier reading, save a page for later viewing, share a web page with other people via email, save a page image to your iPhone, and much more.

Scrolling a Web Page

The iPhone's screen, although large compared to most mobile phones, is still relatively small compared to notebook screens and desktop monitors. This means that for the vast majority of web pages you visit, the entire page will not fit entirely inside the iPhone screen. That's not as big a problem as you might think because your iPhone's touchscreen makes it easy to bring different sections of the page into view by scrolling. Here are the techniques to use:

- **Scroll down:** To scroll down the page, flick toward the top of the screen.

- **Scroll up:** To scroll up the page, flick toward the bottom of the screen.

- **Jump to the top:** To scroll immediately to the top of the page, tap the iPhone status bar.

- **Scroll right:** To scroll the page to the right, flick toward the left side of the screen.

- **Scroll left:** To scroll the page to the left, flick toward the right side of the screen.

> To reduce the amount of left and right scrolling on some web pages, turn your iPhone to the landscape orientation (where the top edge of the iPhone now appears to the left or right). Doing so will give you a wider view of the web page.

Zooming a Web Page

Unless you have extremely sharp vision, or if you've scrolled to the section of the web page you want to read or view, chances are the text or image will be too small. Again, that's not a big hurdle to overcome because your iPhone's touchscreen lets you zoom in on the page for more comfortable viewing. Here are the techniques to try out:

- **Zoom in:** Place your thumb and forefinger together on the touchscreen, centered on the text or image you want to view. Slowly spread your thumb and forefinger apart until the text or image is the size you want.

- **Zoom out:** Place your thumb and forefinger apart on the touchscreen, centered on the text or image you want to view. Slowly pinch your thumb and forefinger together until the text or image is the size you want.

- **Double-tap:** If the web page has separate sections of text, or if it has images, you can quickly zoom a text section or image to the width of the iPhone's screen by double-tapping the text or image. To return to the previous magnification, double-tap the text or image again.

Saving a Web Page as a Bookmark

If you have a web page that you visit regularly, constantly entering the page's address or searching for the page is time-consuming and unproductive. If you visit the page often, you'll likely be able to load it from the History list, but that too can take several taps, and you can't count on the page remaining in the History list if you don't visit it for a few days.

A much better solution is to save the web page as a *bookmark*. Just like a real-world bookmark that you use to save your spot in a book, a bookmark is Safari's way of saving a spot on the Web. When you add a page to Safari's Bookmarks list, you can then revisit the site any time you want with just a few taps.

 **LET ME TRY IT**

Saving a Web Page as a Bookmark

1. Navigate to the web page you want to save as a bookmark.

2. Tap the Actions icon (pointed out earlier in Figure 4.1). Safari displays a menu of commands.

3. Tap Add Bookmark. Safari displays the Add Bookmark screen, shown in Figure 4.6.

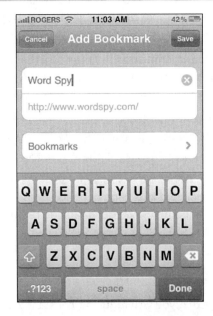

Figure 4.6 *Use the Add Bookmark screen to save a bookmark for an often-visited web page.*

4. Edit the page name, if necessary.

5. Tap Save. Safari adds the page to the Bookmarks list.

To open a bookmarked page, tap the Bookmarks icon (refer back to Figure 4.1), and then tap the bookmark.

Synchronizing Bookmarks

If you've already spent some time organizing your list of bookmarks on your Mac or PC, you probably want those same bookmarks on your iPhone, but you don't want to re-create them all by hand. Fortunately, you don't have to. Instead, you can use iTunes to synchronize your computer bookmarks with your iPhone.

 **LET ME TRY IT**

Synchronizing Bookmarks

1. Connect your iPhone to your Mac or Windows PC.

2. In the iTunes sidebar, click your iPhone in the Devices branch. iTunes displays the Summary tab.

3. Click the Info tab.

4. If you're using a Mac, activate the Sync Safari Bookmarks check box, as shown in Figure 4.7. If you're using a Windows PC, activate the Sync Bookmarks With check box, and then use the list to select your Windows web browser.

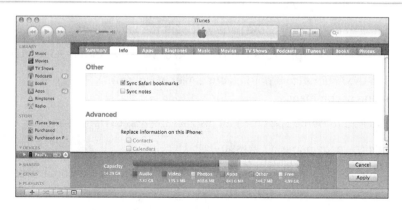

Figure 4.7   *On your Mac, activate the Sync Safari Bookmarks check box.*

5. Click Apply. iTunes synchronizes your computer's bookmarks to your iPhone.

6. When the sync is complete, click the Eject icon next to your iPhone's name in the iTunes Devices list.

Adding a Web Page to the Home Screen

If you have a web page that you visit quite often—for example, a news site or a weather page—you could save that site as a bookmark for easy access. However, "easy" access in this case means loading Safari, accessing the Bookmarks list, and then opening the page. For pages you visit often, that can still seem like a lot of work. For the easiest access to a page, you can save that page to your iPhone Home screen, which means you can surf to that page with just a single tap. Note, too, that Safari automatically opens the page using the location within the page and the zoom level that were set when you saved the page to your Home screen.

 SHOW ME   **Media 4.1—A Video About Adding a Web Page to the Home Screen**
Access this video file through your registered Web Edition at my.safaribooksonline.com/9780132182805/media.

 **LET ME TRY IT**

Adding a Web Page to the Home Screen

1. Surf to the page you want to save.

2. Scroll to the section of the page you want to read or view.

3. Zoom in on the page until you can read or view the content comfortably.

4. Tap the Actions icon (pointed out earlier in Figure 4.1). Safari displays a menu of commands.

5. Tap Add to Home Screen. Safari displays the Add to Home screen.

6. Edit the page name, if necessary.

7. Tap Add. Your iPhone creates an icon for your page in the Home screen.

Sending a Web Page Link via Email

It's not unusual to come across a web page that you want to share with a friend or colleague. You might think the best way to do that is to copy the page address and then paste the address into an email message. Actually, you're right that an email message is the best way to share a link to a page, but you don't have to bother with all that copying and pasting. Instead, you can get your iPhone to do all the work for you.

 **LET ME TRY IT**

Sending a Web Page Link via Email

1. Surf to the page you want to save.

2. Tap the Actions icon (pointed out earlier in Figure 4.1). Safari displays a menu of commands.

3. Tap Mail Link to this Page. Your iPhone creates a new email message and includes the page address in the message body, as shown in Figure 4.8.

Figure 4.8 *Tap Actions and then tap Mail Link to this Page to create a new email message with the page address in the body.*

4. Specify the recipient of the message.

 *To learn how to compose an email message on your iPhone, **see** "Creating and Sending an Email Message," p. 83.*

5. Tap Send. Your iPhone sends the message.

Saving a Web Page Image to Your iPhone

If you come across a web page image that you like, you can save a copy of that image to your iPhone. Note, however, that most web page images are the intellectual property of the website owner, so any images you save can't be used for commercial purposes without permission from the owner.

 LET ME TRY IT

Saving a Web Page Image to Your iPhone

1. Surf to the page that contains the image.

2. Scroll the image into view.

3. Tap and hold on the image. After a couple of seconds, Safari displays a menu of commands.

4. Tap Save Image. Safari saves the image to your iPhone's Camera Roll album. (To view the image, display the Home screen, tap Photos, and then tap Camera Roll.)

Working with Online Forms

Many web pages include or consist of a *form*, which is a collection of interactive controls such as text boxes, check boxes, radio buttons, and lists. You fill in a form to provide a website with information, such as login data, account details, or tech support particulars. When you access an online form, your iPhone displays a special screen that makes it easy for you to fill in the data. You can also activate your iPhone's AutoFill feature that enables you to have some form data entered automatically to save time.

SHOW ME   **Media 4.2—A Video About Filling in Online Forms**
Access this video file through your registered Web Edition at my.safaribooksonline.com/9780132182805/media.

LET ME TRY IT

Filling In a Form

1. Surf to the page that contains the form.

2. Tap the first form control. Safari displays its form interface.

3. Fill in the control data. If the control is a text box, use the onscreen keyboard to tap the text. If the control is a check box or radio button, tap the control to activate it. If the control is a list, flick the scroll wheel up or down to find the item you want (see Figure 4.9), and then tap the item.

Figure 4.9   *To help you choose a list item, Safari displays a scroll wheel, which you flick up and down to navigate the list items.*

4. If the current control is a text box or list, tap Next to display the next form control. If the current control is a check box or radio button, tap the next control you want to work with.

5. Repeat steps 3 and 4 until you've completed the form.

6. Tap Done. Safari returns you to the page, where you can now submit the form.

LET ME TRY IT

Using AutoFill to Save Form Data

1. In the Home screen, tap Settings. Your iPhone opens the Settings screen.

2. Tap Safari. The Safari screen appears.

3. Tap AutoFill to open the AutoFill screen.

4. Tap the Use Contact Info switch to the On position, and then tap your contact item in the Contacts list that appears. This tells Safari to use your Contacts app data to fill in form data.

5. If you want Safari to remember the usernames and passwords you use to log in to sites, tap the Names and Passwords switch to the On position.

TELL ME MORE   **Media 4.3—Understanding the AutoFill Security Risks**

To listen to a free audio recording about the security risks associated with using AutoFill, log on to my.safaribooksonline.com/9780132182805/media.

This chapter shows you how to use your iPhone's Mail app to work with email accounts and to send and receive email messages.

5

Sending and Receiving Email Messages

You might associate email activities with your desktop or notebook computer, but your iPhone frees email from the shackles of the home or office. With your iPhone's Mail app, you can send and receive email messages no matter where you are. Waiting for an important message? With your iPhone, you can still run out for coffee or go shopping, safe in the knowledge that you won't miss anything. Thinking of sending a friend or colleague a message? With your iPhone, even if you're out on the town, you can send that message right away.

This chapter introduces you to your iPhone's Mail app. You learn how to synchronize your email accounts from your computer to your iPhone; add new accounts to your iPhone; compose and send messages; and get, read, and manage incoming messages.

Synchronizing Email Accounts

It's likely that you've got at least one email account already set up in either your Mac's Mail application or your Windows PC's email program (such as Microsoft Outlook). If so, it's also likely that you want to use that same account on your iPhone. You can create email accounts directly on the iPhone (as described in the next section), but it's a lot easier to use iTunes to synchronize your email account with your iPhone.

 **LET ME TRY IT**

Synchronizing Email Accounts

1. Connect your iPhone to your Mac or Windows PC.

2. In the iTunes sidebar, click your iPhone in the Devices branch. iTunes displays the Summary tab.

3. Click the Info tab.

4. If you're using a Mac, activate the Sync Mail Accounts check box, as shown in Figure 5.1. If you're using a Windows PC, activate the Sync Mail Accounts From check box and then use the list to select your Windows email program.

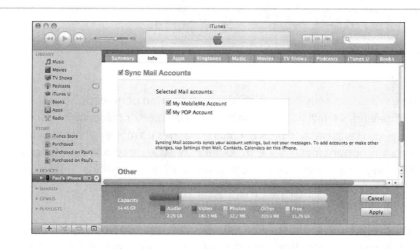

Figure 5.1   *On your Mac, activate the Sync Mail Accounts check box.*

5. Activate the check box beside each email account you want to synchronize with your iPhone.

6. Click Apply. iTunes synchronizes your computer's email accounts to your iPhone.

7. When the sync is complete, click the Eject icon next to your iPhone's name in the iTunes Devices list.

Working with Email Accounts

You can work with email accounts directly on your iPhone. In particular, you can use your iPhone to create a new email account, edit an existing email account, and delete an existing email account. The next few sections provide you with the details.

Creating a New Email Account

You learned earlier in this chapter that the easiest way to get one or more email accounts onto your iPhone is to sync them from your Mac or PC. However, synchronizing email accounts isn't always the best solution. For example, you might have an account that you want to use exclusively on your iPhone. Similarly, you might want to use an existing account on your iPhone when you're not near your computer to perform the sync. Whatever the reason, you can use your iPhone to create the email account by hand. The next few sections take you through the specifics of creating the seven account types supported by the iPhone: MobileMe, Gmail, Yahoo!, AOL Mail, Microsoft Exchange, POP, and IMAP.

TELL ME MORE   Media 5.1—Understanding POP and IMAP Email
Accounts

To listen to a free audio recording about the differences between POP and IMAP accounts, log on to my.safaribooksonline.com/9780132182805/media.

LET ME TRY IT

Creating a New MobileMe Account

MobileMe is the online service maintained by Apple at http://www.me.com. If you have a MobileMe account, follow these steps to configure your iPhone:

1. In the iPhone Home screen, tap Settings. The Settings app appears.

2. Tap Mail, Contacts, Calendars. Your iPhone opens the Mail, Contacts, Calendars screen.

3. Tap Add Account. The Add Account screen appears.

4. Tap the MobileMe logo. Your iPhone displays the MobileMe screen.

5. Use the Name box to enter your name.

6. Use the Address box to enter your MobileMe email address.

7. Use the Password box to enter your MobileMe account password.

8. (Optional) Use the Description box to enter a short description of the account. Figure 5.2 shows a MobileMe account ready to add.

9. Tap Next. Your iPhone contacts the MobileMe service to verify your account. Your iPhone then displays the MobileMe screen shown in Figure 5.3, which lists the data you can sync between MobileMe and your iPhone.

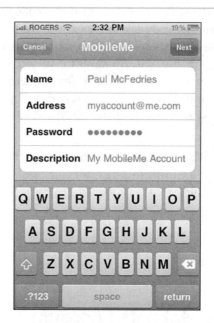

Figure 5.2   *For a MobileMe account, provide your name, address, and password.*

Figure 5.3   *Besides email, you can synchronize contacts, calendars, bookmarks, and notes between MobileMe and your iPhone.*

10. Make sure the Mail switch is set to On. If you want to sync other data between MobileMe and your iPhone, tap the corresponding switches to On.

11. Tap Save.

 **LET ME TRY IT**

Creating a New Gmail Account

1. In the iPhone Home screen, tap Settings. The Settings app appears.

2. Tap Mail, Contacts, Calendars. Your iPhone opens the Mail, Contacts, Calendars screen.

3. Tap Add Account. The Add Account screen appears.

4. Tap the Gmail logo. Your iPhone displays the Gmail screen.

5. Use the Name box to enter your name.

6. Use the Address box to enter your Gmail email address.

7. Use the Password box to enter your Gmail account password.

8. (Optional) Use the Description box to enter a short description of the account.

9. Tap Next. Your iPhone contacts Google to verify your account. Your iPhone then displays the Gmail screen shown in Figure 5.4, which lists the data you can sync between your Google account and your iPhone.

10. Make sure the Mail switch is set to On. If you want to sync other data between Google and your iPhone, tap the corresponding switches to On.

11. Tap Save.

 **LET ME TRY IT**

Creating a New Yahoo! Mail Account

1. In the iPhone Home screen, tap Settings. The Settings app appears.

2. Tap Mail, Contacts, Calendars. Your iPhone opens the Mail, Contacts, Calendars screen.

Figure 5.4 *Besides email, you can synchronize calendars and notes between Google and your iPhone.*

3. Tap Add Account. The Add Account screen appears.

4. Tap the Yahoo! logo. Your iPhone displays the Yahoo! screen.

5. Use the Name box to enter your name.

6. Use the Address box to enter your Yahoo! email address.

7. Use the Password box to enter your Yahoo! account password.

8. (Optional) Use the Description box to enter a short description of the account.

9. Tap Next. Your iPhone contacts Yahoo! to verify your account. Your iPhone then displays the Yahoo! screen shown in Figure 5.5, which lists the data you can sync between your Yahoo! account and your iPhone.

10. Make sure the Mail switch is set to On. If you want to sync other data between Yahoo! and your iPhone, tap the corresponding switches to On.

11. Tap Save.

Figure 5.5   *Besides email, you can synchronize calendars and notes between Yahoo! and your iPhone.*

 LET ME TRY IT

Creating a New AOL Mail Account

1. In the iPhone Home screen, tap Settings. The Settings app appears.

2. Tap Mail, Contacts, Calendars. Your iPhone opens the Mail, Contacts, Calendars screen.

3. Tap Add Account. The Add Account screen appears.

4. Tap the AOL logo. Your iPhone displays the AOL screen.

5. Use the Name box to enter your name.

6. Use the Address box to enter your AOL email address.

7. Use the Password box to enter your AOL account password.

8. (Optional) Use the Description box to enter a short description of the account.

9. Tap Next. Your iPhone contacts AOL to verify your account. Your iPhone then displays the AOL screen shown in Figure 5.6, which lists the data you can sync between your AOL account and your iPhone.

Figure 5.6   *Besides email, you can synchronize notes between AOL and your iPhone.*

10.   Make sure the Mail switch is set to On. If you also want to sync notes between AOL and your iPhone, tap the Notes switch to On.

11.   Tap Save.

 LET ME TRY IT

Creating a New Microsoft Exchange Account

1.   In the iPhone Home screen, tap Settings. The Settings app appears.

2.   Tap Mail, Contacts, Calendars. Your iPhone opens the Mail, Contacts, Calendars screen.

3.   Tap Add Account. The Add Account screen appears.

4.   Tap the Microsoft Exchange logo. Your iPhone displays the Exchange screen.

5.   Use the Email box to enter your Exchange email address.

6.   Use the Domain box to enter your Exchange domain name (if any).

7.   Use the Username box to enter your Exchange account username.

8. Use the Password box to enter your Exchange account password.

9. (Optional) Use the Description box to enter a short description of the account.

10. Tap Next. Your iPhone contacts the Exchange server to verify your account. If your iPhone can verify your account, skip to step 13. If it can't verify the account, it displays a revised version of the Exchange screen with a new Server field.

11. Use the Server box to enter the address of your Exchange server.

12. Tap Next. Your iPhone once again contacts the Exchange server to verify your account. Your iPhone then displays the Exchange Account screen shown in Figure 5.7, which lists the data you can sync between your Exchange account and your iPhone.

Figure 5.7 *Besides email, you can synchronize contacts and calendars between Exchange and your iPhone.*

13. Make sure the Mail switch is set to On. If you want to sync other data between Exchange and your iPhone, tap the corresponding switches to On.

14. Tap Save.

LET ME TRY IT

Creating a New IMAP Account

An IMAP (Internet Message Access Protocol) account is most often used with web-based email services. If you have an account with a different IMAP service (such as Microsoft's Hotmail or Live.com), follow these steps:

1. In the iPhone Home screen, tap Settings. The Settings app appears.

2. Tap Mail, Contacts, Calendars. Your iPhone opens the Mail, Contacts, Calendars screen.

3. Tap Add Account. The Add Account screen appears.

4. Tap Other. Your iPhone displays the Other screen.

5. Tap Add Mail Account. Your iPhone displays the Add Account screen.

6. Use the Name box to enter your name.

7. Use the Address box to enter your Gmail email address.

8. Use the Password box to enter your Gmail account password.

9. (Optional) Use the Description box to enter a short description of the account.

10. Tap Next. Your iPhone contacts the IMAP server to verify your account and then adds the account.

LET ME TRY IT

Creating a New POP Account

A POP (Post Office Protocol) account is common with Internet service providers, and it works by storing incoming messages temporarily on the provider's mail server; you then connect to that server to download your messages. POP accounts also require an outgoing message server to handle the messages you send. Therefore, before setting up your POP account on your iPhone, make sure you know your email address, account password, and the host names of your provider's incoming and outgoing message servers.

To set up a POP account on your iPhone, follow these steps:

1. In the iPhone Home screen, tap Settings. The Settings app appears.

2. Tap Mail, Contacts, Calendars. Your iPhone opens the Mail, Contacts, Calendars screen.

3. Tap Add Account. The Add Account screen appears.

4. Tap Other. Your iPhone displays the Other screen.

5. Tap Add Mail Account. Your iPhone displays the Add Account screen.

6. Use the Name box to enter your name.

7. Use the Address box to enter your POP email address.

8. Use the Password box to enter your POP account password.

9. (Optional) Use the Description box to enter a short description of the account.

10. Tap Next. Your iPhone tries to verify the account data but fails and then displays the Enter Your Account screen

11. Tap POP.

12. In the Incoming Mail Server section, use the Host Name box to enter the host name of your provider's incoming mail server, as well as your user-name and password.

13. In the Outgoing Mail Server section, use the Host Name box to enter the host name of your provider's outgoing mail server. If your provider requires a username and password to send messages, enter those, as well.

14. Tap Save. Your iPhone verifies your account and then adds the account.

Editing an Email Account

After you've added an email account to your iPhone, whether by syncing the account from your computer or by adding the account directly on your iPhone, you shouldn't need to make any changes to the account. However, you might want to change your display name or the account description; or for accounts such as MobileMe, Gmail, Yahoo!, AOL, and Microsoft Exchange, you might want to change which data gets synced to your iPhone.

If you have multiple email accounts on your iPhone, you should tell your iPhone which one to use as the default when you send messages. On the Home screen, tap Settings, Mail, Contacts, Calendars, Default Account, and then tap the account you want to use as the default.

LET ME TRY IT

Editing an Email Account

1. On the Home screen, tap Settings to launch the Settings app.

2. Tap Mail, Contacts, Calendars. Your iPhone opens the Mail, Contacts, Calendars screen.

3. Tap the account you want to edit. Your iPhone displays the account information.

4. If you're editing a MobileMe, Gmail, Yahoo!, AOL, or Microsoft Exchange account, you can use the initial screen to change the sync settings. To edit the account data, tap Account Info.

5. Edit the account data, as required.

6. Tap Done. Your iPhone saves the account data.

Deleting an Email Account

If you have an email account that you no longer use, you should remove that account from your iPhone to save storage space and to make the Mail app easier to navigate.

If you want to stop using the account only temporarily, you can disable the account instead of deleting it. On the Home screen, tap Settings, tap Mail, Contacts, Calendars, and then tap the account you want to disable. For a POP or IMAP account, tap the Account switch to Off. For other account types, tap each sync button to Off.

LET ME TRY IT

Deleting an Email Account

1. On the Home screen, tap Settings to launch the Settings app.

2. Tap Mail, Contacts, Calendars. Your iPhone opens the Mail, Contacts, Calendars screen.

3. Tap the account you want to delete.

4. At the bottom of the screen, tap Delete Account. Your iPhone asks you to confirm.

5. Tap Delete Account.

Sending Messages

Once you have your email account (or accounts) configured on your iPhone, you're ready to start sending out messages to friends, family, or colleagues. Your iPhone makes it easy to compose new messages, and you can even create a custom signature.

 **LET ME TRY IT**

Creating and Sending an Email Message

1. On the Home screen, tap Mail to launch the Mail app, which displays the Inbox for your default email account. If you have only one account on your iPhone, or if you want to send the message using the default account, skip to step 4.

2. Tap the button that appears in the upper-left corner of the Mail app screen. Mail displays the Mailboxes screen.

3. Tap the account you want to use to send the message. Mail displays the account's Inbox screen.

4. Tap the New Message icon, which appears in the lower-right corner of the screen. Mail opens the New Message screen, shown in Figure 5.8.

5. In the To field, type the address of the message recipient; then tap Return. Alternatively, tap the Add (+) button on the right side of the To field to display your Contacts list and then tap the contact you want to use as the recipient. (If the contact has multiple email addresses, you also need to tap the address you want to use.)

Tap and hold the dot (.) key to see a list of keys with common domain name suffixes, such as .com and .edu.

Figure 5.8   *Use the New Message screen to compose your email message.*

6. To add a courtesy copy (Cc) recipient, tap Cc/Bcc, enter the address in the Cc field, and then tap Return. You can also tap Add (+) to select a recipient from your Contacts list.

7. To add a blind courtesy copy (Bcc) recipient, enter the address in the Bcc field and then tap Return. You can also tap Add (+) to select a recipient from your Contacts list.

8. If you want to include multiple recipients in the To, Cc, or Bcc field, repeat steps 5, 6, and 7 as often as necessary.

9. Use the Subject field to enter a subject line for your message.

10. Use the large text area below the Subject field to type your message.

11. Tap Send. The Mail app sends your message.

LET ME TRY IT

Customizing Your Email Signature

By default, the Mail app includes the line "Sent from my iPhone" at the bottom of each new message. This is the default message signature, but you can create a custom signature by following these steps:

1. On the Home screen, tap Settings to open the Settings app.

2. Tap Mail, Contacts, Calendars to display the Mail, Contacts, Calendars screen.

3. Tap Signature. Your iPhone displays the Signature screen, as shown in Figure 5.9.

Figure 5.9 *Use the Signature screen to create a custom message signature.*

4. To start your custom signature from scratch, tap Clear.

5. Type your custom signature into the large text area.

6. Press the Home button to return to the Home screen.

Receiving and Managing Messages

You can also use your iPhone to receive and store incoming messages, which enables you to stay in touch even when you're running errands or traveling. Your iPhone not only lets you read your incoming messages, but it also lets you reply to or forward the messages, save an email image, and delete messages.

Checking for New Messages

How your iPhone checks for new messages depends on the type of mail account:

- **Push:** Some email services—particularly MobileMe and Microsoft Exchange—support *push*, which means those services automatically send new messages to your iPhone as they're received on the server. By default, your iPhone has push turned on.

- **Fetch:** All other email services support *fetch*, where new messages must be requested from the server. By default, your iPhone fetches new messages when you open an account's Inbox using the Mail app, but you must manually fetch new messages if you continue to use that account in the Mail app.

To configure how often your iPhone checks for messages, tap the Home screen's Settings icon, tap Mail, Contacts, Calendars, and then tap Fetch New Data. If you don't want your iPhone to receive push messages, tap the Push switch to Off. For all other accounts, use the Fetch area to tap the interval you want, such as Every 15 Minutes.

 **LET ME TRY IT**

Manually Fetching New Messages

1. On the Home screen, tap Mail to launch the Mail app, which displays the Inbox for your default email account. If you have only one account on your iPhone, or if you want to fetch messages using the default account, skip to step 3.

2. Tap the button that appears in the upper-left corner of the Mail app screen. Mail displays the Mailboxes screen.

3. Tap the Refresh icon, which appears in the lower-left corner of the screen. Mail checks for messages for all your accounts and then downloads any that

are waiting, as shown in Figure 5.10. (Note, too, that if you're working in an account's Inbox, you can also click the Refresh icon in that screen to fetch just that account's messages.)

Refresh icon

Figure 5.10   *Tap the Refresh icon to fetch new messages for your account.*

Reading Messages

After you've received the incoming email messages on your iPhone, you can use the Mail app to read those messages. The Mail app lets you read messages for just a single account or for all your accounts, and it also organizes messages by *thread*, which is the original message and all the replies to that message that you've received.

SHOW ME   Media 5.2—A Video About Reading Email Messages on
Your iPhone

Access this video file through your registered Web Edition at
my.safaribooksonline.com/9780132182805/media.

 **LET ME TRY IT**

Reading Messages

1. On the Home screen, tap Mail to launch the Mail app, which displays the Inbox for your default email account. If you have only one account on your iPhone, or if you want to read messages using the default account, skip to step 4.

2. Tap the button that appears in the upper-left corner of the Mail app screen. Mail displays the Mailboxes screen.

3. If you want to read messages for all your accounts, tap All Inboxes. Otherwise, tap the account you want to work with. Mail displays the messages, as shown in Figure 5.11. Note that unread messages are marked with a blue dot and threads appear with a number on the right that tells you how many messages are in the thread.

Figure 5.11 *Tap an account to see its messages, or tap All Inboxes to read all your messages from every account.*

4. Tap the message you want to read. If you tapped a thread, Mail displays a list of the messages in the thread. Otherwise, Mail displays the message; in this case, skip to step 6.

5. If you opened a thread, tap the thread message you want to read. Mail displays the message.

6. To navigate the messages, tap the Next and Previous icons in the upper-right corner (see Figure 5.12).

Figure 5.12   *Once you have a message displayed, use the Next and Previous controls to navigate your messages.*

If you're reading a thread, to read other messages, tap the button in the upper-left corner until you return to the list of messages and then tap the next message you want to read.

If you'd prefer not to read messages in threads, you can turn off this feature. On the Home screen, tap Settings, tap Mail, Contacts, Calendars, and then tap the Organize by Thread switch to Off.

Replying to a Message

Many of the messages you receive on your iPhone will be "read-only" and so won't require further action from you. However, if the sender asks you a question or requests information, comments, or other feedback, you can send back a response right from your iPhone.

Replying to a Message

1. On the Home screen, tap Mail to launch the Mail app, which displays the Inbox for your default email account. If you have only one account on your iPhone, or if you want to reply to a message in the default account, skip to step 4.

2. Tap the button that appears in the upper-left corner of the Mail app screen. Mail displays the Mailboxes screen.

3. Tap the account that contains the message you want to work with. Mail displays the account's Inbox screen.

4. Tap the message you want to reply to. Mail opens the message.

5. Tap the Actions icon, which is the left-pointing arrow in the toolbar at the bottom of the screen (refer to Figure 5.12). Mail displays a list of commands.

6. Tap Reply. Mail creates a new message, adds the sender to the To field, fills in the Subject field with the original subject line preceded by Re:, and adds the original message text to the bottom of the message box.

> If you want the reply to go to the sender and every person included in the To and Cc fields, click Reply All, instead.

7. Type a message to the sender.

8. Edit the original message, if necessary.

9. Tap Send. The Mail app sends your reply.

Forwarding a Message

If you receive a message that you think might be of interest to another person, you can forward the message to that person.

Forwarding a Message

1. On the Home screen, tap Mail to launch the Mail app, which displays the Inbox for your default email account. If you have only one account on your iPhone, or if you want to forward a message from the default account, skip to step 4.

2. Tap the button that appears in the upper-left corner of the Mail app screen. Mail displays the Mailboxes screen.

3. Tap the account that contains the message you want to forward. Mail displays the account's Inbox screen.

4. Tap the message you want to forward. Mail opens the message.

5. Tap the Actions icon (pointed out in Figure 5.12). Mail displays a list of commands.

6. Tap Forward. Mail creates a new message, fills in the Subject field with the original subject line preceded by Fwd:, and adds the original message text to the bottom of the message box.

7. In the To field, type the address of the message recipient, and then tap Return. Alternatively, tap the Add (+) button on the right side of the To field to display your Contacts list, and then tap the contact you want to use as the recipient. (If the contact has multiple email addresses, you also need to tap the address you want to use.)

8. Type a message to the sender.

9. Edit the original message, if necessary.

10. Tap Send. The Mail app forwards the message.

Saving an Email Image to Your iPhone

The mail app supports photos and other images in email messages. Occasionally you might receive a message with a photo or other picture that you want to keep, either to store on your iPhone or, if you have a Mac, to sync to the iPhoto application. In such cases, you can save a copy of an image directly from the email message.

SHOW ME   Media 5.3—A Video About Saving an Image from an Email
Message
Access this video file through your registered Web Edition at
my.safaribooksonline.com/9780132182805/media.

 LET ME TRY IT

Saving an Email Image to Your iPhone

1. On the Home screen, tap Mail to launch the Mail app, which displays the
   Inbox for your default email account. If you have only one account on your
   iPhone, or if you want to work with a message from the default account,
   skip to step 4.

2. Tap the button that appears in the upper-left corner of the Mail app
   screen. Mail displays the Mailboxes screen.

3. Tap the account that contains the message you want to work with. Mail
   displays the account's Inbox screen.

4. Tap the message that contains the image. Mail opens the message.

5. Tap and hold the image. Mail displays a list of commands, as shown in
   Figure 5.13.

Figure 5.13   *Tap and hold an email image to see this list of actions.*

6. Tap Save Image. The Mail app saves the image to your iPhone's Camera Roll.

⊕ *To learn how to view photos on your iPhone,* **see** *"Viewing Photos," p. 164.*

Deleting Messages

If you have one or more messages that you no longer need or that didn't interest you in the first place, you should delete those messages. Doing so reduces clutter in the email accounts Inbox, makes the message list easier to navigate, and frees up disk space on your iPhone. In addition to that, there are also performance issues if your iPhone contains a large number of images/videos/etc.

 LET ME TRY IT

Deleting Email Messages

1. On the Home screen, tap Mail to launch the Mail app, which displays the Inbox for your default email account. If you have only one account on your iPhone, or if you want to delete messages from the default account, skip to step 4.

2. Tap the button that appears in the upper-left corner of the Mail app screen. Mail displays the Mailboxes screen.

3. Tap the account that contains the messages you want to delete. Mail displays the account's Inbox screen.

4. Tap Edit. Mail enables the Inbox editing tools.

5. For each message you want to delete, tap the selection circle to the left of the message. Mail displays a white checkmark on a red background, as shown in Figure 5.14.

6. Tap Delete. The Mail app deletes the selected messages.

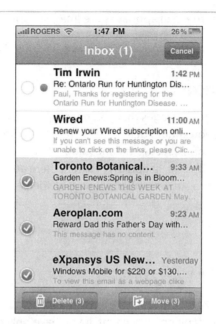

Figure 5.14   *Tap Edit and then select the messages you want to delete.*

In this chapter, you learn how to synchronize, play, and download music using your iPhone.

6

Managing Music on Your iPhone

You might think that your iPhone is good for "practical" tasks such as surfing the Web, exchanging messages, and making phone calls, but for "fun" tasks such as playing music you'd be better off with a device designed for that purpose, such as an iPod. Surprisingly, that's not the case at all! Your iPhone not only comes with an iPod app that many people think is better than the iPod itself, but it also comes with an iTunes app that lets you find, sample, and download songs and albums right on your phone. This chapter shows you how to synchronize music with your computer and then shows you how to use the iPod and iTunes apps.

Synchronizing Music

You will see later in this chapter (in the "Downloading Music Using the iTunes App" section) that you can download songs and albums right from the comfort of your iPhone. However, there's a good chance that you've already used iTunes on your Mac or Windows PC to create a collection of music, either by copying (or *ripping*, in the vernacular) songs from audio CDs or by purchasing songs from the iTunes Store. If so, you probably want to put some or all of that collection on your iPhone. Fortunately, this is readily done because you can use iTunes to synchronize your computer's music with your iPhone.

There are two ways you can go about this:

 TELL ME MORE   Media 6.1—Understanding Your Music Syncing Options
To listen to a free audio recording about your iTunes music syncing options, log on to my.safaribooksonline.com/9780132182805/media.

- **Sync everything:** This is the easiest way to go because you can set it up with just a couple of mouse clicks. However, you need to make sure you have enough free space on your iPhone to handle your complete music collection.

To tell whether your music collection will fit on your iPhone, first get the total size of your collection by clicking the Music category in the iTunes sidebar and then reading the size value in the status bar. Then connect your iPhone, click the phone in iTunes' Devices list, and read the amount of free space you have.

- **Sync some:** This method means that you send some of your music to your iPhone, which is the way to go if your computer's music collection is too big to fit on your iPhone, or if you only want certain music on your iPhone. You determine what gets synced by selecting specific playlists, artists, and genres. If you want to go the playlist route, be sure to create all the playlists you require before doing the sync.

 LET ME TRY IT

Synchronizing Music

1. Connect your iPhone to your Mac or Windows PC.

2. In the iTunes sidebar, click your iPhone in the Devices branch. iTunes displays the Summary tab.

3. Click the Music tab.

4. Activate the Sync Music check box.

5. If you want to sync your entire music collection to your iPhone, click the Entire Music Library option; if you need (or prefer) to sync only part of your collection, skip to step 9. Click the Selected Playlists, Artists, and Genres option, instead (see Figure 6.1), and proceed with step 6.

6. In the Playlists list, activate the check box beside each playlist you want to sync to your iPhone.

7. In the Artists list, activate the check box beside each artist you want to sync to your iPhone.

8. In the Genres list, activate the check box beside each genre you want to sync to your iPhone.

9. Click Apply. iTunes synchronizes your computer's music to your iPhone.

10. When the sync is complete, click the Eject icon next to your iPhone's name in the iTunes Devices list.

Figure 6.1   *Activate the Sync Music check box and then sync either your entire music library or selected playlists, artists, and genres.*

Playing Music Using the iPod App

I mentioned earlier that many people consider the iPhone's iPod app to be a superior music player than the iPod device itself. How can that be? It's all about the interface. The iPod app takes full advantage of the iPhone's slick and easy-to-use touch interface, so finding, navigating, and playing music is easier than ever, particularly compared to the (relatively) clunky click wheel on traditional iPods. (I say "traditional" because the iPod touch has a Music app with a touch interface that's almost identical to the iPhone's iPod app.) In this section, you learn how to use the iPod app's interface to navigate your music, play tunes, create playlists, and more.

Navigating the iPod App

To get started with the iPod app, tap the iPod icon in the Home screen's dock. In the iPod app screen, you see five icons in the menu bar at the bottom of the screen:

- **Playlists:** Tap this icon to display the Playlists screen, which shows the playlists you synchronized to your iPhone. You can also use the Playlists screen to create new playlists, as I describe later in this chapter (see "Creating a Playlist" and "Creating a Genius Playlist").

- **Artists:** Tap this icon to display the Artists screen, which shows the artists that are currently on your iPhone (see Figure 6.2). Tap an artist to see that artist's albums, and then tap an album to see its songs. (If an artist only has a single album on your iPhone, tapping the artist takes you directly to that album's songs.)

Figure 6.2   *Tap the Artists icon in the menu bar to see a list of the artists currently on your iPhone.*

- **Songs:** Tap this icon to display the Songs screen, which shows the songs that are currently on your iPhone.

- **Videos:** Tap this icon to display the Videos screen, which shows the music videos or movies currently on your iPhone.

- **More:** Tap this icon to display the More screen (see Figure 6.3), which offers seven media categories, including the music-related categories Albums, Compilations (multiple-artist albums), Composers, and Genres.

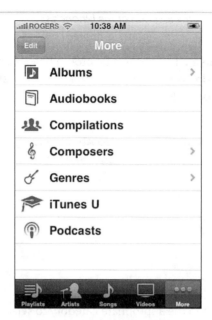

Figure 6.3   *Tap More to see the seven media categories shown here.*

If you use one of the More categories frequently, you can add it to the menu bar for easier access. Tap More, tap Edit, tap and drag the icon you want to add, and then drop it on the icon you want to replace. Tap Done to complete the edit.

Playing Music

Now that you have some tunes on your iPhone and you're familiar with the iPod app, you're ready to start playing music. Before getting to the specifics of playing music, you first need to decide on the audio output device. You have three choices:

- **iPhone speaker:** If you have no headphones, you can play back the music through your iPhone's built-in speaker, which is located on the bottom edge of the phone. Point the bottom of the iPhone toward you for best sound quality.

- **Regular headset:** If you have a headset with a stereo mini-jack connector (such as the headset that comes with your iPhone), connect it to the headset jack on the top edge of the iPhone.

*For more information on the location of the iPhone's speaker and headset jack, **see** "Getting to Know the Rest of the iPhone," (Chapter 1).*

- **Bluetooth headset:** If you have a Bluetooth headset, pair the headset with your iPhone, as described later in this chapter (see "Listening to Music through a Bluetooth Headset").

 SHOW ME   **Media 6.2—A Video About Playing Music on the iPhone**
Access this video file through your registered Web Edition at my.safaribooksonline.com/9780132182805/media.

 **LET ME TRY IT**

Playing Music

1. In the iPod app, tap the appropriate category to select your music.

2. If the category offers subcategories, tap the subcategory you want. For example, after you tap an artist, composer, or genre, you may then need to tap the album you want to hear.

3. Tap the song you want to hear. The iPod app begins playing the song and displays the album art (if any), as shown in Figure 6.4.

4. To control the volume, press the iPhone's volume buttons on the side of the phone, tap and drag the Volume slider on the playback screen, or press the volume buttons on the iPhone headset.

5. To temporarily suspend the playback, tap the Play/Pause button on the playback screen, or press the center button on your iPhone headset. To resume, tap the Play/Pause button or press the center button on your iPhone headset.

6. To fast-forward the current song, tap and hold the Next/Fast-forward button or press the center button on your iPhone headset twice quickly and hold the button after the second press; to skip the current song, tap the Next/Fast-forward button, or press the center button on your iPhone headset twice quickly.

7. To rewind the current song, tap and hold the Previous/Rewind button or press the center button on your iPhone headset three times quickly and hold the button after the third press; to return to the beginning of the current song, tap the Previous/Rewind; to go to the previous song, tap the Previous/Rewind button twice, or press the center button on your iPhone headset three times quickly.

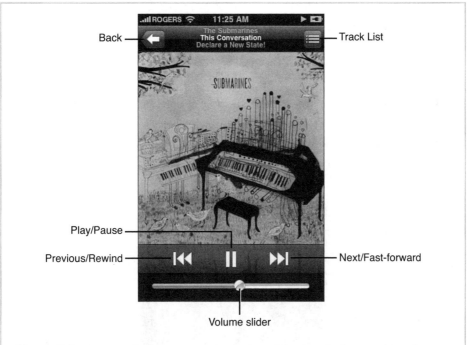

Figure 6.4 *Locate and then tap a song to play it, and then use the features shown here to control the playback.*

8. To switch to another song, tap the Track List button to see the list of songs in the current album or playlist and then tap the song you want to hear.

You can switch to a random song in the current album or playlist by giving your iPhone a vigorous shake. To turn this function on or off, go to Settings, Music, Shake to Shuffle.

Playing Music via Voice Commands

If you've got lots of music on your iPhone and you know exactly what you want to hear, it might take you a while to locate the specific playlist, artist, or album. In such cases, it's often easier to use the Voice Control feature, which comes with the iPhone 4 and 3GS. With Voice Control, you just tell the iPhone what you want to hear, and it locates the playlist, artist, or album automatically and begins playing.

 **LET ME TRY IT**

Playing Music via Voice Commands

1. Tap and hold the Home button. The Voice Control screen appears, as shown in Figure 6.5.

2. Wait until you hear two beeps. This tells you that Voice Control is ready to receive your next command.

Figure 6.5 *Press and hold the Home button to display the Voice Control screen.*

3. Very clearly speak "play," "playlist," "artist," or "album," and then say the name of the playlist, album, or artist. The iPod app begins playing the music.

4. To control the playback, tap and hold the Home button to display the Voice Control screen; wait for the beeps; and then say "pause," "play," "next song," or "previous song."

Listening to Music Through a Bluetooth Headset

For wireless listening, you can pair your iPhone with a Bluetooth headset and listen to your music through the headset. In most cases, your iPhone automatically sets up the paired Bluetooth headset as the audio output device. If that doesn't happen with your headset, you need to know how to select it as the output device.

To learn how to pair a Bluetooth headset with your iPhone, **see** *"Pairing Your Phone to a Bluetooth Headset," (Chapter 3).*

 LET ME TRY IT

Listening to Music Through a Bluetooth Headset

1. Pair your Bluetooth headset with your iPhone.

2. Open the iPod app and play the music you want to hear.

3. In the playback screen, tap the Bluetooth icon, which appears to the right of the Volume slider (see Figure 6.6). The iPod app displays a list of the available output devices (usually just your Bluetooth headset and the iPhone's built-in speaker), as shown in Figure 6.6.

4. Tap Bluetooth Audio. The iPod app begins playing the music through the Bluetooth headset

Creating a Playlist

It's usually best to create playlists using iTunes on your Mac or Windows PC, because your computer gives you access to your complete music collection. However, if you're away from your computer and you need a playlist right away for an upcoming event, such as a workout or walk, you can use the iPod app to create a playlist from the music on your iPhone.

 SHOW ME   **Media 6.3—A Video About Creating a Playlist**
Access this video file through your registered Web Edition at my.safaribooksonline.com/9780132182805/media.

Bluetooth icon

Figure 6.6   *In the playback screen, tap the Bluetooth icon, and then tap Bluetooth Audio play your music through the Bluetooth headset.*

 **LET ME TRY IT**

Creating a Playlist

1. In the iPod App, tap Playlists. The Playlists screen appears.

2. Tap Add Playlist. The iPod app displays the New Playlist dialog box.

3. Type the name of your playlist, and then tap Save. The iPod app displays the Songs screen.

4. For each song you want to include in the playlist, tap the song. The iPod app marks the chosen songs by displaying them in a lighter text color, as shown in Figure 6.7.

5. Tap Done. The iPod app displays the playlist screen, where you can click Edit to add or remove the songs, Clear to remove all songs, or Delete to remove the playlist.

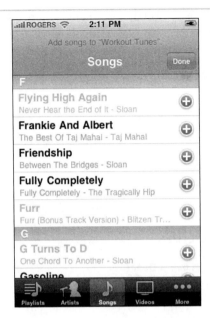

Figure 6.7 *Tap each song you want to include in your playlist, and the iPod app displays the selected tracks in a lighter text color.*

Creating a Genius Playlist

As you saw in the previous section, creating a playlist directly on your iPhone is straightforward, although it can take some time depending on how many songs you want in the playlist. If you need to create a playlist as quickly as possible, or if you want to explore a particular type of music, you can get the iPod app to create a playlist for you automatically. This is called a Genius playlist, and it's "smart" because you pick a song on your iPhone, and the iPod app builds an automatic playlist of songs that are similar.

 **LET ME TRY IT**

Creating a Playlist

1. In the iPod App, tap Playlists. The Playlists screen appears.

2. Tap Genius Playlist. The iPod app displays the Songs screen.

3. Tap the song you want to use as the basis for the Genius playlist. The iPod app creates the playlist and starts playing it.

4. Tap the Back button (pointed out earlier in Figure 6.4). The iPod app displays the list of songs in the playlist, as shown in Figure 6.8.

5. Tap Save. The iPod app saves the Genius playlist under the name of the original song you selected.

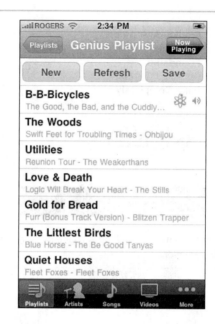

Figure 6.8   *Tap Playlists, tap Genius Playlist, and then tap a song to create a playlist of similar tunes.*

If you later add more songs to your iPhone, you can update the Genius playlist by tapping Playlists, tapping the Genius playlist, and then tapping Refresh.

Downloading Music Using the iTunes App

Accessing the iTunes Store through your Mac or Windows PC is the easiest way to locate music and to keep your music purchases and other downloaded media organized. However, if you're out and about with your iPhone and you hear or think of a song or album you want right away, you can use the iTunes app on your iPhone to locate, sample, and purchase the music. Later, when you sync your iPhone with your computer, your purchased music gets transferred automatically to the desktop version of iTunes.

Navigating the iTunes Store

To get started with the iTunes app, tap the iTunes icon in the Home screen. In the iTunes app screen, you see five icons in the menu bar at the bottom of the screen:

- **Music:** Tap this icon to display the main screen of the mobile version of the iTunes Store, shown in Figure 6.9. Tap New Releases to see the latest albums added to the store; tap Top Tens to see a list of the top sellers in various categories; and tap Genres to browse music using categories such as Alternative, Country, and Jazz.

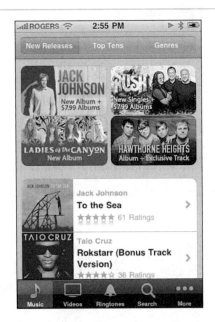

Figure 6.9   *Tap the Music icon to begin browsing the iTunes Store.*

- **Videos:** Tap this icon to display the Videos section of the store, and tap the buttons at the top of the screen to access the three subsections: Movies, TV Shows, and Music Videos.

- **Ringtones:** Tap this icon to browse ringtones for your phone, which are organized into three sections: Featured, Top Tens, and Genre.

- **Search:** Tap this icon to search for music on the iTunes Store (see "Searching for Music," later in this chapter).

- **More:** Tap this icon to display the More screen (see Figure 6.10), which offers four more categories: Podcasts, Audiobooks, iTunes U, and Downloads.

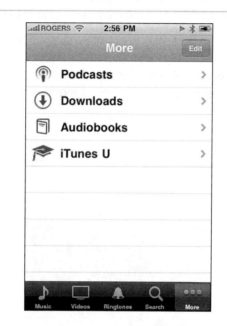

Figure 6.10 *Tap More to see the four extra iTunes categories shown here.*

If you find yourself frequently using one of the categories in the More screen, add it to the menu bar for easier access. Tap More, tap Edit, tap and drag the icon you want to add, and then drop it on the icon you want to replace. Tap Done to complete the edit.

Searching for Music

The Music section of the iTunes Store and its three subsections (New Releases, Top Tens, and Genres) are a great way to browse for new music and to locate new artists. However, if you know exactly what you want—whether it's a particular artist, album, or song—trying to find the music by browsing can be frustrating and time-consuming because the iTunes Store contains millions of songs. A much faster and easier method is to search for the specific artist, album, or song that you want to purchase.

 **LET ME TRY IT**

Searching for Music

Follow these steps to search for music using the iTunes app:

1. In the iTunes app, tap the Search icon. iTunes displays the Search screen.

2. Tap inside the Search box. The onscreen keyboard appears.

3. Type a word or phrase from the name of the artist, album, or song you want to locate.

4. Tap Search. iTunes displays the search results, as shown in Figure 6.11.

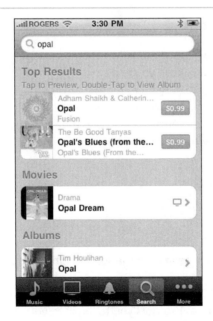

Figure 6.11   *Tap Search, type your search text, and then tap Search to see the results, which are organized as shown here.*

Sampling Music

One of the great features of the iTunes Store is that it gives you instant access to thousands of artists and millions of songs that you might never otherwise come across. It's a great way to expand your music horizons, but how can you be sure you'll like a particular artist or song? Honestly, you can never be absolutely certain that you'll like the new music you purchase, but the iTunes Store helps by allowing you to sample any song for free. It's only a 30-second clip for each song, but that's usually enough to decide whether you dislike a song, and it's often enough to decide that you like a song enough to purchase it.

 **LET ME TRY IT**

Sampling Music

1. Either browse to or search for the song you want to sample.

2. Tap the song. iTunes begins playing the sample.

3. If you want to stop the preview before it finishes, tap the song.

Purchasing Music

If you've found the music you're looking for and, optionally, sampled the music to have some idea that you like it, you're ready to purchase the music and have it downloaded to your iPhone. Remember that any music you purchase on your iPhone gets transferred automatically to your Mac or Windows PC the next time you sync. iTunes sets up a special category in the Store section of the sidebar called Purchased on *iPhone*, where *iPhone* is the name of your iPhone.

 **LET ME TRY IT**

Purchasing Music

1. Either browse to or search for the song or album you want to purchase.

2. Tap the price. The price button changes to a Buy Now button.

3. Tap Buy Now. iTunes prompts you to log in to your iTunes Store account.

4. Type your iTunes Store username and password. In subsequent purchases, you only have to type your password.

5. Tap OK. iTunes begins downloading the music.

6. To watch the progress of the download, tap More, and then tap Downloads (see Figure 6.12).

Figure 6.12 *After you purchase your music, tap More and then tap Downloads to watch the progress of the download.*

After you've made at least one purchase from the iTunes Store, the iTunes app adds a Purchased item to the Playlists screen. Tap Playlists and then Purchased to see a list of the albums and songs you've bought on your iPhone.

This chapter shows you how to use the Contacts app, including how to create new contacts and how to edit existing contacts.

7

Managing Contacts on Your iPhone

Your iPhone comes with a Contacts app that you use to store information about people and companies. The Contacts app is useful not only for viewing data about your friends, family, and colleagues, but it also help to simplify and speed up tasks in other apps. For example, rather than typing someone's email address when you're sending a message with the Mail app, you can just select that person's address from your list of contacts. Similarly, you can also use your list of contacts to select a phone number using the Phone app, view a person's website using the Safari app, and see a map for a person's home or business using the Maps app.

To ensure you're getting the most out of Contacts and all the iPhone apps that use it, this chapter shows you how to synchronize contacts with your computer, create new contacts, edit existing contacts, and delete contacts you no longer need.

Synchronizing Contacts

You see in the rest of the chapter that you can use your iPhone's Contacts app to create new contacts right on your iPhone. However, if you've already got a list of contacts going on your computer or online, you can use iTunes to synchronize your contacts with your iPhone. The contacts list you use depends either on the operating system you use or which online service you use:

- **Mac OS X:** Use your Mac's Address Book application.

- **Windows:** If you have Microsoft Office installed, use the Outlook application; if you have Windows Live Mail installed, use the Windows Live Contacts application; otherwise, use the Windows Contacts application.

- **Online:** If you maintain your contacts online, you can use either your Google contacts or your Yahoo! contacts.

 **LET ME TRY IT**

Synchronizing Contacts

1. Connect your iPhone to your Mac or Windows PC.

2. In the iTunes sidebar, click your iPhone in the Devices branch. iTunes displays the Summary tab.

3. Click the Info tab.

4. If you're using a Mac, activate the Sync Address Book Contacts check box, as shown in Figure 7.1. If you're using a Windows PC, activate the Sync Contacts With check box, and then use the list to select your Windows contacts program (such as Outlook).

Figure 7.1   *On your Mac, activate the Sync Address Book Contacts check box.*

5. If you want to sync your entire address book to your iPhone, leave the All Contacts option selected. Otherwise, click Selected Groups, and then activate the check box beside each group you want to synchronize with your iPhone.

6. If you want the contacts you create on your iPhone to get synced to your computer, activate the Add Contacts Created Outside of Groups on this iPhone To check box, and then choose a group from the menu.

7. On a Mac, if you also want your Yahoo! Address Book contacts synced, activate the Sync Yahoo! Address Book Contacts check box, type your Yahoo! ID and password, and click OK.

8. On a Mac, if you also want your Google Contacts synced, activate the Sync Google Contacts check box, type your Google username and password, and click OK.

9. Click Apply. iTunes synchronizes your computer's contacts to your iPhone.

10. When the sync is complete, click the Eject icon next to your iPhone's name in the iTunes Devices list.

Creating a New Contact

Although syncing your computer's contacts to your iPhone is by far the easiest way to populate the Contacts app, it's by no means the only way. If you meet a new friend while you're away from your computer or if a colleague gives you his or her contact data, you can create a new contact right on your iPhone. Depending on how much data you have to enter, this can be fairly laborious, so I've divided the process into separate tasks for each type of information: phone numbers, email addresses, website addresses, a contact's photo, and so on. Each of them uses the New Contact screen shown in Figure 7.2.

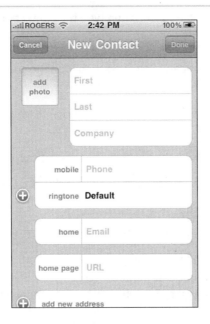

Figure 7.2   *In the Contacts app, tap the Add icon (+) to open the New Contact screen.*

Another way to create a new contact on your iPhone is to have a person send you an electronic business card (sometimes called a vCard) by email. Open the email message on your iPhone, tap the attached card, and then tap Create New Contact.

 LET ME TRY IT

Starting a New Contact

1. In the Home screen, tap the Contacts icon. Your iPhone launches the Contacts app.

2. By default, Contacts adds new people to the All Contacts list. This is proba-bly the way you want to go, but if you need to change this, tap Groups and then tap the list or group you want to use.

3. Tap the Add icon (+), which appears in the upper-right corner of the Contacts screen. The Contacts app displays the New Contact screen, shown in Figure 7.2.

4. Tap inside the First field, and then type the contact's first name.

5. Tap inside the Last field, and then type the contact's last name.

6. Tap inside the Company field, and then type the contact's first company name (if any).

 LET ME TRY IT

Adding a Phone Number to a Contact

1. Tap the Phone field.

2. Type the contact's phone number.

3. Tap the label to the left of the phone number field. (The default label for the first phone number is mobile.) The Contacts app displays the Label screen, shown in Figure 7.3, which lists all the labels you can assign to the phone number.

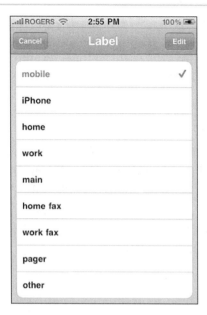

Figure 7.3 *Use the Labels screen to assign a label that aptly describes the contact's phone number.*

If you don't see an appropriate label, tap Add Custom Label, type the label you want to use, and then tap Save.

4. Tap the label you want to use for the phone number. The Contacts app applies the new label and then creates new Phone field.

5. To add other phone numbers for the contact, repeat steps 1 to 4 for each new Phone field.

 TELL ME MORE **Media 7.1—Understanding the Usefulness of Contact Labels**

To listen to a free audio recording about why field labels are useful, log on to my.safaribooksonline.com/9780132182805/media.

If you want your new contact to have a distinct ringtone, tap the Ringtone field to open the Ringtones screen, tap the sound you want your iPhone to play when this contact calls you, and then tap Save.

Adding an Email Address to a Contact

1. Tap the Email field.

2. Type the contact's email address.

3. Tap the label to the left of the Email field. (The default label for the first email address is home. The Contacts app displays the Label screen, which lists all the labels you can assign to the email address.)

4. Tap the label you want to use for the email address. The Contacts app applies the new label and then creates new Email field.

5. To add other email addresses for the contact, repeat steps 1 to 4 for each new Email field.

Adding a Web Page Address to a Contact

1. Tap the URL field.

2. Type the contact's web page address.

3. Tap the label to the left of the URL field. (The default label for the web page address is home page.) The Contacts app displays the Label screen, which lists all the labels you can assign to the web page address.

4. Tap the label you want to use for the web page address. The Contacts app applies the new label and then creates new URL field.

5. To add other web page addresses for the contact, repeat steps 1 to 4 for each new URL field.

Adding a Street Address to a Contact

1. Tap Add New Address. The Contacts app displays the Street, City, State, ZIP, and Country fields, as shown in Figure 7.4.

Figure 7.4   *Tap Add New Address to display the address fields shown here.*

2. Tap the Street field and then type the contact's street address.

3. Tap the second Street field, and then type the rest of the contact's street address, if any.

4. Tap the City field, and then type the contact's city.

5. Tap the State field, and then type the contact's state or province.

6. Tap the ZIP field, and then type the contact's ZIP code or postal code.

7. Tap the Country field to open the Country screen, and then tap the contact's country.

8. Tap label to the left of the first Street field. (The default label for the first offline address is home.) Then use the Label screen to tap the label you want to use for the offline address.

9. To add other offline addresses for the contact, repeat steps 1 to 8 for each address.

 SHOW ME   **Media 7.2—A Video About Assigning a Photo to a Contact**
Access this video file through your registered Web Edition at
my.safaribooksonline.com/9780132182805/media.

 **LET ME TRY IT**

Assigning a Photo to a Contact

1. At the top of the New Contact screen, tap Add Photo. The Contacts app asks whether you want to take a photo now or choose an existing photo.

2. Tap Choose Photo. Your iPhone opens the Photo Albums screen.

Figure 7.5 *After you tap the photo you want to assign to the contact, use the Move and Scale screen to pan to and zoom in on the portion of the image you want to use.*

3. Tap the album that contains the photo you want to use.

4. Tap the photo you want to assign to the contact. Your iPhone displays the Move and Scale screen, shown in Figure 7.5.

5. Spread you fingers on the photo to zoom in to the magnification you want to use.

6. Drag the image to bring into view the portion of the image you want to use.

7. Tap Choose. The Contacts app assigns the photo to the contact.

LET ME TRY IT

Adding Other Fields to a Contact

1. Tap Add Field. The Contacts app displays the Add Field screen, which lists all the extra fields you can add.

2. Tap the field you want to add. The Contacts app adds the field to the New Contact screen.

3. Type the data for the new field.

4. If the field accepts a label, tap the label to the left of the field to open the Label screen, and then tap the label you want to use for the field.

5. To add other fields for the contact, repeat steps 1 to 4 as needed.

LET ME TRY IT

Completing the New Contact

1. Recheck the data you entered to ensure that it's complete and accurate.

2. Tap Done. The Contacts app saves the new contact and opens the Info screen, which displays the contact's data.

3. Tap All Contacts to returns to the All Contacts list.

Editing a Contact

Whether you've synced your contact data with your computer, got contact data pushed to your iPhone from your MobileMe account, or created new contacts yourself, you can make changes to any contact stored on your iPhone. This is useful if you realize that there's an error in a contact's information, if a contact is missing data, or if a contact's information changes.

SHOW ME   Media 7.3—A Video About Editing a Contact

Access this video file through your registered Web Edition at my.safaribooksonline.com/9780132182805/media.

LET ME TRY IT

Editing a Contact

1. In the Home screen, tap the Contacts icon. Your iPhone launches the Contacts app.

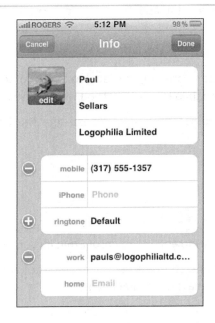

Figure 7.6 *Display the contact and then tap Edit to open the data for editing.*

2. Tap the contact you want to edit. The Contacts app opens the Info screen.

3. Tap Edit. The Contacts app opens the contact data for editing, as shown in Figure 7.6.

4. To make changes to existing data, tap inside the field and then edit the field contents.

5. To add a new field, tap inside an empty field of the data type you want to add (such as Phone or Email) and then type the new data.

6. To remove a field, tap the red Delete icon to the left of the field and then tap the Delete button that appears.

7. When you've completed your edits, tap Done. The Contacts app saves the modified data.

Deleting a Contact

If you have a contact you no longer need, it's a good idea to delete that contact. This makes the contacts list easier to navigate and slightly reduces the disk space used by the Contacts app.

 LET ME TRY IT

Deleting a Contact

1. In the Home screen, tap the Contacts icon. Your iPhone launches the Contacts app.

2. Tap the contact you want to remove. The Contacts app opens the contact's Info screen.

3. Tap Edit. The Contacts app opens the contact data for editing.

4. Tap Delete Contact. The Contacts app asks you to confirm.

5. Tap Delete Contact. The Contacts app removes the contact.

This chapter shows you how to use your iPhone's time-related features, including the Calendar app and the Clock app.

8

Tracking Appointments and Events

You might think of your iPhone as a "communication" device that enables you to make calls and exchange messages; as an "information" device that enables you to surf the Web and navigate the world; and as an "entertainment" device that enables you to listen to music, view photos, and watch movies. However, your iPhone is also a "life" device that helps you keep your affairs in order, even when you're on the go. You saw in Chapter 7, "Managing Contacts on Your iPhone," that your iPhone's Contacts app makes it easy to view, create, and edit data about the people you know. In this chapter, you see how your iPhone can help you maintain your schedule. With the Calendar app you can monitor, add, and edit upcoming events, and with the Clock app, you can set alarms, run timers, and more.

Synchronizing Calendars

You see later in this chapter that you can use your iPhone's Calendar app to create new events right on your iPhone. However, if you've already got a calendar or two going, either in your Mac's iCal application or in Microsoft Outlook on your Windows computer, you can use iTunes to synchronize your computer calendars with your iPhone.

 LET ME TRY IT

Synchronizing Calendars

1. Connect your iPhone to your Mac or Windows PC.

2. In the iTunes sidebar, click your iPhone in the Devices branch. iTunes displays the Summary tab.

3. Click the Info tab.

4. If you're using a Mac, activate the Sync iCal Calendars check box, as shown in Figure 8.1. If you're using a Windows PC, activate the Sync Calendars

With check box, and then use the list to select your Windows contacts program (such as Outlook).

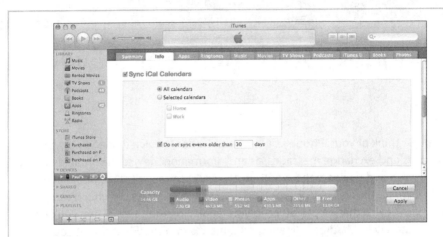

Figure 8.1   *On your Mac, activate the Sync iCal Calendars check box.*

5.   If you want to sync all your events to your iPhone, leave the All Calendars
     option selected; otherwise, click Selected Calendars, and then activate the
     check box beside each calendar you want to synchronize with your
     iPhone.

6.   Click Apply. iTunes synchronizes your computer's calendars to your iPhone.
     If you added or changed any events on your iPhone, those changes are
     also synced to your computer.

7.   When the sync is complete, click the Eject icon next to your iPhone's name in
     the iTunes Devices list.

Navigating the Calendar

To work with your calendars on your iPhone, you use the Calendar app, which you
launch by tapping the Calendar icon in the Home screen. Figure 8.2 shows a typical
Calendar screen.

To navigate the calendar, you use the three view buttons at the bottom of the
Calendar screen:

- **Month:** This view shows one month at a time, as you can see in Figure 8.2.
  Dates that have a least one scheduled event are displayed with a dot below

Figure 8.2   *Tap the Calendar icon to open the Calendar app and view or modify your schedule.*

the date. Use the right and left arrows on either side of the month to display the next and previous months, respectively. Tap a day to view its scheduled events below the calendar.

- **Day:** This view shows one day at a time, as you can see in Figure 8.3. Use the right and left arrows on either side of the date to display the next and previous days, respectively. If a day has scheduled events, they appear as blocks in the timeline.

- **List:** This view shows a list of your upcoming events, as shown in Figure 8.4.

In any view, you can immediately jump to today's scheduled events by tapping the Today button.

Adding Events to the Calendar

Although it's usually easiest to create new events using a computer application such as iCal or Outlook, you might remember or learn of an event that needs scheduling while you're away from your computer. Instead of jotting down the details on a piece of paper, you can create the new event right away on your iPhone.

Figure 8.3 *Tap Day to view your scheduled events one day at a time.*

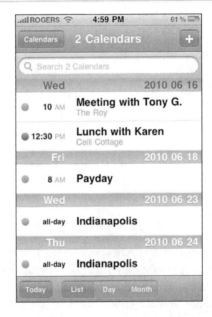

Figure 8.4 *Tap List to see a list of your upcoming scheduled events.*

Adding a Basic Event

A "basic" event is one that requires only the minimum amount of data, which means an event name and the date and time when the event starts. You can also specify a location, an end time, and notes about the event.

 LET ME TRY IT

Adding a Basic Event

1. In the iPhone Home screen, tap Calendar to open the Calendar app.

2. Navigate to the date on which the event occurs.

3. Tap the Add (+) icon. Calendar displays the Add Event screen.

4. Tap the Title box. Calendar displays the Title & Location screen.

5. Tap the Title box and then type the event title.

6. (Optional) Tap the Location box and type the event location.

7. Tap Done. Calendar returns you to the Add Event screen.

8. Tap the Starts/Ends box. Calendar displays the Start & End screen, shown in Figure 8.5.

9. Tap Starts, and then use the time wheel to set the starting time for the event.

10. Tap Ends, and then use the time wheel to set the ending time for the event.

11. Tap Done.

12. If you have multiple calendars, tap Calendar, tap the calendar in which you want to display your event, and then tap Done.

If you have one calendar that you use for most of your events, you should set up that calendar as the default. In the iPhone Home screen, tap Settings, tap Mail, Contacts, Calendars, tap Default Calendar, and then tap the calendar you want to use as the default.

13. If you want to add notes about the event, tap Notes, type your text, and then tap Done. Figure 8.6 shows a new event ready to be added.

14. Tap Done. Calendar saves the event and adds it to the calendar.

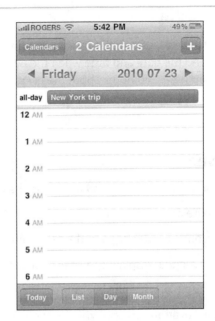

Figure 8.5   *Use the Start & End screen to set the starting and ending times of your event.*

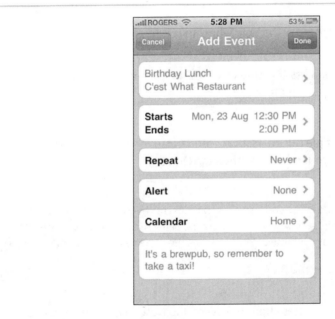

Figure 8.6   *A basic event, ready to be saved.*

To make changes to an event, navigate to the date when the event occurs, tap the event, and then tap Edit.

Adding an All-Day Event

An all-day event is one that has no set start or end time, such as a birthday or an anniversary. All-day events can also be multiple-day affairs, such as a conference, sales meeting, or vacation. In the Day view, all-day events appear above the time-line, so you can still add events to that day (such as conference appointments or vacation activities).

 LET ME TRY IT

Adding an All-Day Event

1. In the iPhone Home screen, tap Calendar to open the Calendar app.

2. Navigate to the date on which the event occurs.

3. Tap the Add (+) icon. Calendar displays the Add Event screen.

4. Specify the basic event data, as described in the "Adding a Basic Event" section.

5. Tap the Starts/Ends box. Calendar displays the Start & End screen.

6. Tap the All-day switch to On. Calendar hides the time controls, as shown in Figure 8.7.

7. If the event runs over multiple days, tap Ends and adjust the ending date for the event.

8. Tap Done.

9. Tap Done. Calendar saves the event and adds it to the calendar. In Day view, the all-day event appears above the timeline, as shown in Figure 8.8.

Adding a Repeating Event

If you have an event that recurs on a regular schedule, don't enter all the future events by hand. Instead, take advantage of Calendar's Repeat Event feature, which enables you to automatically repeat an event every day, every week, every two weeks, every month, or every year.

Figure 8.7   *To designate this as an all-day event, tap the All-day switch to On.*

Figure 8.8   *All-day events appear above the timeline in Day view.*

SHOW ME   Media 8.1—A Video About Adding a Repeating Event
Access this video file through your registered Web Edition at
my.safaribooksonline.com/9780132182805/media.

 **LET ME TRY IT**

Adding a Repeating Event

1. In the iPhone Home screen, tap Calendar to open the Calendar app.

2. Navigate to the date on which the event occurs.

3. Tap the Add (+) icon. Calendar displays the Add Event screen.

4. Specify the basic event data, as described in the "Adding a Basic Event" section.

5. Tap Repeat. Calendar displays the Repeat Event screen, shown in Figure 8.9.

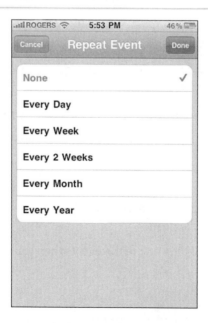

Figure 8.9   *Tap Repeat to open the Repeat Event screen, and then choose the recurrence you want to apply for to event.*

6. Tap the recurrence you want to use for the event.

7. Tap Done.

8. Tap Done. Calendar saves the event and adds the recurrences to the calendar.

Adding an Alert to an Event

Recording your upcoming events digitally is only useful if you remember to check your schedule. However, it's when you're at your busiest that it's the hardest to remember to see what's coming up. Fortunately, your iPhone can help here. The Calendar app offers an Alert feature that displays a message and plays a sound when an event is approaching. For good measure, you can even add a second alert to ensure you don't miss your appointment.

 **LET ME TRY IT**

Adding an Alert to an Event

1. In the iPhone Home screen, tap Calendar to open the Calendar app.

2. Navigate to the date on which the event occurs.

3. Tap the Add (+) icon. Calendar displays the Add Event screen.

4. Specify the basic event data, as described in the "Adding a Basic Event" section.

5. Tap Alert. Calendar displays the Event Alert screen, shown in Figure 8.10.

6. Tap the amount of time before the event when you want the alert to appear.

7. Tap Done.

8. If you want to create another reminder for the event, tap Second Alert. The Event Alert screen appears.

9. Tap the amount of time before the event when you want the second alert to appear.

10. Tap Done.

11. Tap Done. Calendar saves the event and later displays the alert (or alerts) at the time (or times) you specified.

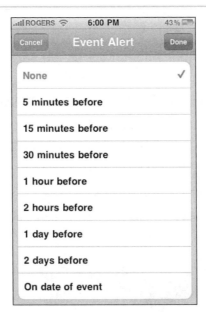

Figure 8.10   *Tap Alert to open the Event Alert screen, and then choose when you want the alert to appear.*

Follow Another Person's Calendar

The Calendar app is useful for keeping track of your own schedule, but sometimes you might also need to keep track of someone else's schedule. It could be your boss, someone you work with, your spouse, or your child. This is possible if the other person has published his or her schedule. For example, in the Mac's iCal application, you can publish a calendar to Apple's MobileMe service. (Click the calendar, and then select Calendar, Publish.) In that case, the person will have an address for the published calendar (usually in the form *server/calendar*.ics, where *server* is name of the server where the calendar is published and *calendar* is the name of the published calendar file). After you have that address, you can subscribe to the calendar using your iPhone, and that person's events will then appear in the Calendar app.

 **LET ME TRY IT**

Follow Another Person's Calendar

1. In the Home screen, tap Settings. The Setting app appears.

2. Tap Mail, Contacts, Calendars. Your iPhone opens the Mail, Contacts, Calendars screen.

3. Tap Add Account. The Add Account screen appears.

4. Tap Other. The Other screen appears.

5. Tap Add Subscribed Calendar. The Subscription screen appears, as shown in Figure 8.11.

Figure 8.11   *Use the Subscription screen to type the address of the published calendar.*

6. Use the Server box to type the address of the published calendar.

7. Tap Next. Your iPhone verifies the address and then displays the subscription configuration screen.

8. Tap Save. Your iPhone creates a new Subscribed Calendar section in the Mail, Contacts, Calendars screen, and adds your subscribed calendar to that section.

If you no longer want to subscribe to a published calendar, tap Settings, tap Mail, Contacts, Calendars, Subscribed Calendars, and then tap the calendar. If you only want to temporarily disable the calendar, tap the Account switch to Off; otherwise, tap Delete Account, and then tap Delete Account again when your iPhone asks you to confirm.

Using Your iPhone's Clock

Your iPhone comes with a Clock app that's remarkably versatile. For example, it can not only show you the current time for a major city or town from anywhere in the world, but can also show you the time from *multiple* cities and towns. You can also use the Clock app as an alarm clock, a stopwatch, and a timer.

To launch the Clock app, tap the Clock icon on your iPhone's Home screen.

Viewing the Current Time in Another City

The Clock app comes with a World Clock feature that enables you to add clocks for cities you deal with regularly. For example, if you're never quite sure what time it is in Newfoundland, Canada, you can add a clock for its capital, St. John's. Similarly, if you regularly do business with people in France, you should add a clock for Paris so that you don't end up calling someone too early or too late.

 **LET ME TRY IT**

Viewing the Current Time in Another City

1. In the iPhone Home screen, tap the Clock icon to open the Clock app.

2. Tap the World Clock icon at the bottom of the screen.

3. Tap the Add (+) icon in the upper-right corner of the screen.

4. Tap inside the Search box, and then begin typing the name of the place you want to add. As you type, the Clock app displays a list of matching places, as shown in Figure 8.12.

5. When you see the city you want to add, tap it. The Clock app adds the city to the World Clock tap. Figure 8.13 shows the World Clock tab with several cities added.

Figure 8.12   *Start typing the name of the city you want to add, and the Clock app displays a list of the matching places.*

In the World Clock tab, a black clock background tells you that it's nighttime at the location; a white clock background indicates daytime.

To remove a clock you no longer need, tap Edit, tap the red Delete (-) icon beside the city, and then tap Delete. Tap Done to exit Edit mode.

Setting an Alarm

The Clock application also comes with an Alarm feature that you can set to have your phone sound an alarm at whatever time you specify, which is handy not only for waking you up in the morning, but also for reminding you of pending tasks. If you want to use your iPhone as an alarm clock, the Clock app comes with a snooze option, just in case you need an extra nine minutes of sleep before you rise and shine.

Figure 8.13   *You can populate the World Clock tab with several cities.*

 TELL ME MORE   **Media 8.2—Understanding Alarms on the iPhone**
To listen to a free audio recording about alarms and your iPhone, log on to
my.safaribooksonline.com/9780132182805/media.

 LET ME TRY IT

Setting an Alarm

1. In the iPhone Home screen, tap the Clock icon to open the Clock app.

2. Tap the Alarm icon at the bottom of the screen.

3. Tap the Add (+) icon in the upper-right corner of the screen. The Add Alarm screen appears, as shown in Figure 8.14.

4. If you want the alarm repeated on a particular day of the week, tap Repeat, tap the day (such as Every Monday), and then tap Back.

5. To set the sound that plays when the alarm goes off, tap Sound, tap the sound effect you want, and then tap Back.

Figure 8.14 *Use the Add Alarm screen to set up your alarm.*

6. If you want the option if tapping the Snooze button when the alarm goes off, tap the Snooze switch to On.

7. To set the title of the dialog that appears when the alarm goes off, tap Label, type the title, and then tap Back.

8. Use the hour, minutes, and AM/PM wheels to set the time you want the alarm to go off.

9. Tap Save. Clock adds the alarm to the Alarm tab and turns it on.

To disable an alarm, tap its On/Off switch to Off. To remove an alarm you no longer use, tap Edit, tap the red Delete (-) icon beside the alarm, and then tap Delete. Tap Done to exit Edit mode.

Timing an Event

If you need to time a race, a phone call, or a cooking procedure, the Clock app comes with a Stopwatch feature that not only lets you time events, but also lets you time individual laps in a race.

SHOW ME   Media 8.3—A Video About Timing an Event
Access this video file through your registered Web Edition at
my.safaribooksonline.com/9780132182805/media.

 LET ME TRY IT

Timing an Event

1. In the iPhone Home screen, tap the Clock icon to open the Clock app.

2. Tap the Stopwatch icon at the bottom of the screen. The Clock app displays the Stopwatch.

3. Tap Start. The timer starts, the Start button turns to a red Stop button, and the Reset button turns to a Lap button, as shown in Figure 8.15.

Figure 8.15 *Use the Clock app's Stopwatch feature to time a race or other event.*

4. If you want to record lap times, tap the Lap key at the end of each lap. Clock adds the time of each lap to the list.

5. When the event is done, tap Stop.

Setting Up a Countdown Timer

The Clock application's Alarm feature is useful if you know what time you want the alarm to go off. However, there are many situations where you want to get a reminder a certain number of minutes or hours from now. Put an egg on to boil, and you might want a reminder in 3 or 4 minutes; decide to take a break from work, and you might want a reminder in 15 minutes. The Clock app comes with a Timer feature, which plays sounds, vibrates the phone, and displays a message after whatever interval you specify.

 **LET ME TRY IT**

Setting Up a Countdown Timer

1. In the iPhone Home screen, tap the Clock icon to open the Clock app.

2. Tap the Timer icon at the bottom of the screen. The Clock app displays the Timer, as shown in Figure 8.16.

Figure 8.16 *Use the Clock app's Timer feature to set up a countdown timer that goes off after a specified number of hours and minutes.*

3. Use the hours and minutes wheels to set the duration of the countdown.

4. To specify the sound that your iPhone plays when the timer counts down to zero, tap When Timer Ends, tap the sound effect you want to use, and then tap Set.

5. When you're ready to begin the countdown, tap Start. The Clock app begins the countdown, displays the remaining time in the Timer tab, and then displays the alert when the countdown reaches zero.

This chapter introduces you to your iPhone's Maps
app and shows you how to use it to find locations
and get directions.

9

Navigating Your World with Maps

Your iPhone comes with a built-in Global Positioning System (GPS) receiver. Combined with the location data supplied by nearby cellular system towers, your iPhone can determine your current location with reasonable accuracy. To take advantage of this, your iPhone also comes with an app called Maps, which comes from Google and its famous Google Maps division. All this means that you can not only use your iPhone to see where you are, but can also locate other places on a map, get directions between any two points, view traffic conditions, and more.

Mapping Locations

As you might imagine from the name, the most straightforward task you can perform with the Maps app is to display locations on a map. This could be your current location, a particular building or address, or the address of someone in your iPhone's Contacts app.

Mapping Your Current Location

If you find yourself in an unfamiliar part of town, or if you're investigating a new city, the best way to get your bearings is to find your current location on a map. With a paper map, that requires looking for nearby intersections and then finding those streets on the map. With your iPhone's Maps app, however, you can locate yourself on a map with a single tap of a button.

In fact, showing you your current location is such a common task that the latest version of the Maps app now shows you your location automatically when you start the app. That is, when you tap the Maps icon in the iPhone's Home screen, the Maps app automatically displays a map of your current area and then homes in your exact location, which it then displays using a blue dot, as shown in Figure 9.1. (If you see a message on screen asking whether Maps can use your current location, be sure to tap OK.)

If you happen to be in a car, bus, or some other moving vehicle, the blue location dot moves right along with you. If you scroll or pan the map so that you can no longer see your current location, you can redisplay it at any time by tapping the Tracking icon, which appears in the lower-left corner of the Maps screen (and is pointed out in Figure 9.1).

Tracking icon

Figure 9.1 *When you launch Maps, the app automatically pinpoints your current location and displays it as a blue dot.*

If you want to *literally* get your bearings, tap the Tracking icon a second time to get into compass mode. In this mode, the Maps screen automatically orients itself to the north. That is, whatever edge of the iPhone is pointing away from you is always pointing north.

Mapping a Place or an Address

If you know the name of the city, neighborhood, company, or building you want to work with, or if you know the specific address, you can enter that information into Maps and it will display the location on a map.

 **LET ME TRY IT**

Mapping a Place or an Address

1. In the Maps app, tap inside the Search or Address box. Maps displays the Search screen.

2. Type the name or address of the location.

> Your searches don't have to be for specific places or addresses. You can perform general searches such as "coffee" and "shopping," and Maps will display pushpins for all the nearby locations that match your search. Tap a pushpin to see more information about the location.

3. Tap Search. The Maps app finds the location, adds a red pushpin to the map to pinpoint the location, and then displays a banner with the location name, as shown in Figure 9.2.

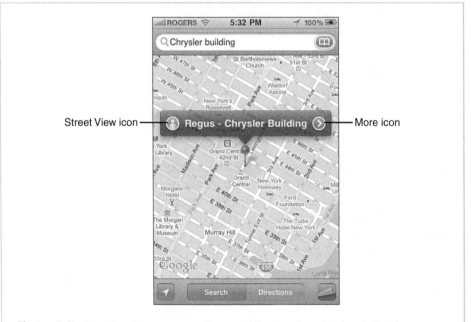

Figure 9.2 *Type the place name or address and then tap Search to locate the place on a map.*

4. If you want to find out more about the location, tap the blue More icon to open the Info screen, which shows data such as the location's phone number, address, and website. When you have finished with the data, tap Map to return to the map.

5. To view an image of the location, tap the red Street View icon. Maps switches to Street View and displays an image of the location. You can pan from side to side by flicking left and right, and you can pan up by flicking down, as shown in Figure 9.3. When you're done with Street View, tap the map icon in the lower-right corner to return to the map.

Figure 9.3   *Tap the Street View icon to see a photo of the location, which you can then pan left and right, up and down.*

Mapping a Contact's Address

You may have street addresses for some of the people or businesses in your iPhone's Contacts app, which might be addresses that you've synced from your computer or added by hand, as described in Chapter 7, "Managing Contacts on Your iPhone." You can take advantage of that data by having the Maps app locate a contact's address on a map, which can be handy if you're visiting the contact for the first time.

To learn how to enter a contact's street address, **see** *"Adding a Street Address to a Contact," p. 118.*

 **LET ME TRY IT**

Mapping a Contact's Address

1. In your iPhone's Home screen, tap Contacts. The Contacts app appears.

2. Tap the contact you want to map. The contact's Info screen appears.

3. Tap the address you want to map. Your iPhone switches to the Maps app, which then displays a pushpin that pinpoints the contact's address, as shown in Figure 9.4.

Figure 9.4   *Open the contact you want to locate, tap the contact's address, and the Maps app locates the address on a map.*

Changing the Map View

You'll most often work with the Maps app using the default Map view, but Maps also comes with three other views you can use. Here's the complete list:

- **Map:** This is the default view, and it shows your locations and other data on a map.

- **Satellite:** This view shows a satellite photo of the current location, as shown in Figure 9.5.

Figure 9.5 *Satellite view shows you a satellite photo for the current map area.*

- **Hybrid:** This view overlays map data such as street names and region names onto the satellite photo.

- **List:** This view displays a list of all the places that have pushpins on the current map.

 **LET ME TRY IT**

Changing the Map View

1. Use the Maps app to bring the location you want to work with into view.

2. Tap the Actions icon (pointed out in Figure 9.6). Maps displays a set of actions and options, as shown in Figure 9.6.

3. Tap the view you want to use: Map, Satellite, Hybrid, or List. Maps switches to the new view and returns you to the map.

Pinning a Location

In many cases, you might want to see a map without knowing the name or address of a specific place. For example, if you're in a new city, you might want to see a map of downtown or of a particular neighborhood. You can do that by panning the map

Figure 9.6   *Tap the Actions icon to see this set of buttons.*

to bring the area into view. However, if you later want to find out how to get from your current location to the area you're looking at (as described later in this chapter), how can you get directions if you don't have a specific location for a destination?

You can work around this problem by *pinning* a location to the map. This means that Maps drops a pushpin into the center of the current map and you then move that pushpin to the location you want. When the pin is where you want, you can get directions, save the location, or send the location to someone (all of which are explained in the next section).

 LET ME TRY IT

Pinning a Location

1. Use the Maps app to bring the area you want to work with into view.

2. Tap the Actions icon (pointed out earlier in Figure 9.6). Maps displays a set of actions and options.

3. Tap Drop Pin. Maps returns you to the map and drops a purple pushpin, which it named Dropped Pin.

4. Tap and drag the Dropped Pin to the location you want. Maps displays the address of the location, as shown in Figure 9.7.

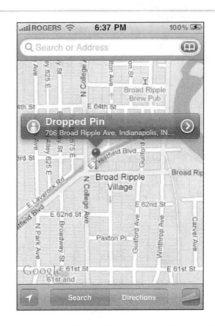

Figure 9.7   *Tap the Actions icon, tap Drop Pin, and then drag the Dropped Pin to the location you want.*

Working with Locations

Once you have a location pinned to a map, the Maps app gives you several ways to work with that location. For example, you can get directions to (or from) that location, you can save the location as a Maps bookmark, you can send a map of the location to another person via email or text message, or you can view the traffic conditions near the location.

Getting Directions to a Location

Knowing where a place is located on a map is one thing, but it's quite another to actually get there, particularly if you're unfamiliar with the area. The Maps app can help by providing you with step-by-step (or, really, turn-by-turn) directions that you can follow to get from your current location (or some other location you specify) to the destination. In many cases, Maps can alternatively supply you with directions for walking or taking transit to the location.

SHOW ME Media 9.1—A Video About Getting Directions to a Location
Access this video file through your registered Web Edition at
my.safaribooksonline.com/9780132182805/media.

 LET ME TRY IT

Getting Directions to a Location

1. Use Maps to add a pushpin for your destination.

2. If you don't see the banner with the location name above the pushpin, tap the pushpin.

3. Tap the blue More icon. The location's Info screen appears.

4. Tap Directions to Here. Maps displays the Directions screen and fills in the location's address in the End box. Maps also displays Current Location in the Start box; if you want to start from your current location, skip to step 6.

5. To begin the directions from a different location, tap the X on the right side of the Start box to clear it, and then type the address.

> If the new start location is one you've looked up recently, tap the blue Bookmarks icon that appears on the right side of the cleared Start box, tap the Recents tab, and then tap the location in the list that appears.

6. Tap Route. The Maps app displays a new map that shows your starting location with a green pushpin, your destination with a red pin, the proposed route between the two locations, and the approximate length and time of the route, as shown in Figure 9.8.

7. Use the icons at the top of the screen to select the type of directions you want: driving, transit, or walking.

8. Tap Start. Maps displays the first step of the route.

9. Follow the instructions and then tap the right arrow to see the next step.

10. Repeat step 9 until you reach your destination.

Figure 9.8 *Specify your starting and ending locations, and then tap Route to see this overview of the directions.*

Saving a Location as a Bookmark

If you find yourself looking up the same place or address frequently, or if you often use a particular address as a starting point for directions, it can be time-consuming to constantly enter the same information, particularly a long address. To save time and effort, you can store that location as a bookmark, which means you can retrieve the information with just a few taps.

 SHOW ME   **Media 9.2—A Video About Saving a Location as a Bookmark**
Access this video file through your registered Web Edition at my.safaribooksonline.com/9780132182805/media.

 **LET ME TRY IT**

Saving a Location as a Bookmark

1. Use Maps to add a pushpin for your destination.

2. If you don't see the banner with the location name above the pushpin, tap the pushpin.

3. Tap the blue More icon. The location's Info screen appears.

4. Tap Add to Bookmarks. Maps displays the Add Bookmark screen.

5. Edit the bookmark name, if necessary.

6. Tap Save. Maps saves the bookmark.

> To select a bookmark, tap the blue Bookmark icon that appears on the right side of the Search box, tap the Bookmarks tab, and then tap your bookmark. To get directions to or from a bookmark, open the Directions screen, tap the blue Bookmark icon that appears on the right side of the Start or End box, tap the Bookmarks tab, and then tap the bookmark.

Sending a Location

If you've located some place that you want to share with another person, you can send the location via email. The message the person receives includes a link that, when clicked, opens a Google Maps page and displays the location.

You can also send a location via text message using Multimedia Messaging Service (MMS). In this case, the message the person receives includes an attached vCard file, which contains information about the location.

 **LET ME TRY IT**

Sending a Location via Email

1. Use Maps to add a pushpin for your destination.

2. If you don't see the banner with the location name above the pushpin, tap the pushpin.

3. Tap the blue More icon. The location's Info screen appears.

4. Tap Share Location. The Share Location Using pop-up appears.

5. Tap Email. Your iPhone creates a new email message, which includes a link to the location in the message body, as shown in Figure 9.9.

6. Select your recipient.

Figure 9.9   *Open the location's Info screen, tap Share Location, and then tap Email to create the new email message with a link to the location.*

7. Add text to the message, if necessary.

8. Tap Send. Your iPhone sends the message.

 **LET ME TRY IT**

Sending a Location via Text Message

1. Use Maps to add a pushpin for your destination.

2. If you don't see the banner with the location name above the pushpin, tap the pushpin.

3. Tap the blue More icon. The location's Info screen appears.

4. Tap Share Location. The Share Location Using pop-up appears.

5. Tap MMS. Your iPhone creates a new text message, which includes an attachment for the location, as shown in Figure 9.10.

6. Select your recipient.

Figure 9.10 *Open the location's Info screen, tap Share Location, and then tap MMS to create the new text message with an attachment for the location.*

7. Add text to the message, if necessary.

8. Tap Send. Your iPhone sends the message.

Viewing Traffic Information

If you want to travel to a location by car or taxi, traffic can slow you down and cause you to be late. You could listen for local radio reports, but the Maps app gives you a much easier method: You can display current traffic conditions right on the map.

For major North American cities, Maps can display traffic information by displaying major roads and highways with one of the following four colors:

*   **Green:** This color applies to routes where the traffic is moving at 50 miles per hour (mph) or faster.

*   **Yellow:** This color applies to routes where the traffic is moving between 25 and 50 mph.

- **Red:** This color applies to routes where the traffic is moving at 25 mph or slower.

- **Gray:** This color applies to routes that currently have no traffic data.

 **LET ME TRY IT**

Viewing Traffic Information

1. Use the Maps app to bring the location you want to work with into view.

2. Tap the Actions icon (pointed out earlier in Figure 9.6). Maps displays a set of actions and options.

3. Tap Show Traffic. Maps displays the traffic conditions, as shown in Figure 9.11.

Figure 9.11   *Tap the Actions icon, and then tap Show Traffic to see the color-coded traffic conditions.*

This chapter shows you how to use your iPhone's camera and how to work with photos on your iPhone.

10

Taking and Viewing Photos

Your iPhone comes with a built-in camera that enables you to quickly take photos no matter where you are. And if you have an iPhone 4, you actually have *two* cameras to play with—the main camera in the rear of the phone and an extra camera in the front of the phone.

The photos you take are stored on your iPhone, and you can later synchronize them to your computer. You can also synchronize your computer's photos to your iPhone. With your phone loaded with pictures, you can then view the photos, run a slide show, and share photos with friends and family.

Synchronizing Photos

You see later in this chapter that you can use your iPhone's built-in camera (or cameras) to take photos right on your iPhone. However, if you've already got some photos on your computer, you can use iTunes to synchronize your computer photos to your iPhone. Conversely, you can also synchronize your iPhone's photos to your computer.

 LET ME TRY IT

Synchronizing Photos from Computer to iPhone

1. Connect your iPhone to your Mac or Windows PC.

2. In the iTunes sidebar, click your iPhone in the Devices branch. iTunes displays the Summary tab.

3. Click the Photos tab.

4. Activate the Sync Photos From check box.

5. If you're using a Mac and you want to synchronize photos from the iPhoto application, select iPhoto in the Sync Photos From pop-up menu.

Otherwise, use the Sync Photos From menu to select the folder that contains the photos you want to sync. If you don't see the folder in the list, click Choose Folder, and then use the dialog box that appears to select the folder you want to use.

6. You now have two ways to proceed, depending on whether you're choosing photos from iPhoto or a folder:

    -   **iPhoto:** If you want to sync all your photos to your iPhone, leave the All Photos, Albums, Events, and Faces option selected. Otherwise, click Selected Photos, Albums, Events, Faces, and then activate the check box beside each album, event, and face you want to synchronize with your iPhone, as shown in Figure 10.1.

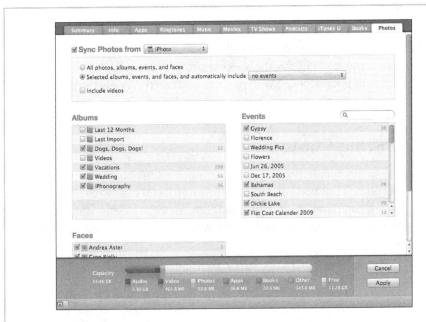

Figure 10.1   *On your Mac, you can use iPhoto to synchronize selected albums, events, and faces.*

    -   **Folder:** If you want to sync all the photos in the selected folder to your iPhone, leave the All Folders option selected. Otherwise, click Selected Folders and then activate the check box beside each subfolder you want to synchronize with your iPhone.

7. Click Apply. iTunes synchronizes your computer's photos to your iPhone.

8. When the sync is complete, click the Eject icon next to your iPhone's name in the iTunes Devices list.

 **LET ME TRY IT**

Synchronizing Photos from iPhone to Mac

1. Connect your iPhone to your Mac. The iPhoto application appears.

2. In the iPhoto sidebar, click your iPhone in the Devices branch. iPhoto displays thumbnail versions of the phone's photos.

3. In the Event Name text box, type a word or short phrase that describes the photos you're importing.

4. If you want to import only some of your iPhone's photos, as shown in Figure 10.2, hold down the Command key and click each photo you want to import.

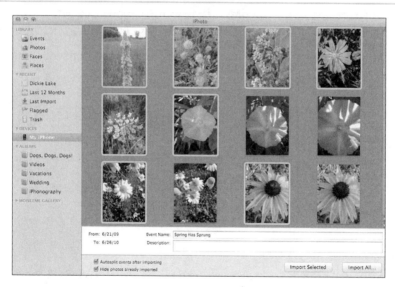

Figure 10.2   *On your Mac, you can use iPhoto to import some or all of your iPhone's photos.*

5. If you're importing only some of your iPhone's photos, click Import Selected; otherwise, click Import All. iPhoto begins importing the photos. When the import is complete, iPhoto asks whether you want to delete the imported photos from your iPhone.

6. If you no longer need to view the photos on your iPhone, click Delete Photos. Otherwise, if you still want the photos on your iPhone, click Keep Photos.

7. In iTunes, click the Eject icon next to your iPhone's name in the Devices list.

 **LET ME TRY IT**

Synchronizing Photos from iPhone to Windows

1. Connect your iPhone to your Windows PC. After a few moments, the AutoPlay window appears.

2. Click Import Pictures and Videos. Windows displays the Import Pictures and Videos dialog box.

3. Type a tag for the photos. A *tag* is a word or short phrase that describes the photos. Note, however, that this step is optional.

4. Click Import. Your Windows PC begins importing the photos.

5. While the import is in progress, if you want Windows to delete the photos after the import is complete, activate the Erase After Importing check box.

6. When the import is complete, disconnect your iPhone from your Windows PC.

> If you've installed Windows Live Photo Gallery on your PC, you can use it to import photos from your iPhone. Connect your phone, open Windows Live Photo Gallery, and then select File, Import From a Camera or Scanner. In the Import Photos and Video window, click your iPhone, and then click Import.

Taking Photos with the Camera

If you have an iPhone 4, the main camera on the back of the phone is 5 megapixels, which means it creates nice, sharp images, and it also includes a built-in LED flash for photographing low-light or dark scenes. The iPhone 4 also comes with a 0.3-megapixel camera on the front, which is useful for taking self-portraits. (The previous-generation iPhone, the 3GS, comes with a single 3-megapixel camera with no LED flash.) Also, the latest iPhone software comes with a 5x digital zoom as well as a tap-to-focus feature.

 TELL ME MORE   Media 10.1—Taking Better Photos with Your iPhone

To listen to a free audio recording about improving your iPhone photos, log on to my.safaribooksonline.com/9780132182805/media.

 **LET ME TRY IT**

Taking a Photo with the Camera

1. In the iPhone Home screen, tap the Camera icon to open the Camera app.

2. To change the zoom level, tap the screen to display the zoom slider, shown in Figure 10.3, and then drag the slider right (to zoom in) or left (to zoom out).

3. (iPhone 4) To choose an LED flash setting, tap the Flash icon in the upper-left corner of the screen, and then tap No (to ensure the flash doesn't go off), Yes (to ensure the flash does go off), or Auto (to let your iPhone determine whether the flash is required).

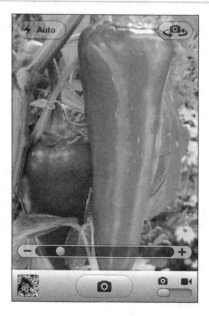

Figure 10.3 *Tap the screen to display the zoom slider, and then drag the slider right or left to set the zoom level.*

4. To focus the image, tap the screen on the spot you want in focus.

5. (iPhone 4) To switch to the front camera, tap the Switch Cameras icon, located in the upper-right corner of the screen.

6. Tap the shutter button in the center of the Camera app toolbar. Your iPhone takes the picture and then displays a thumbnail version of the photo in the lower-left corner.

If you want to see the photo you just took, tap the thumbnail of the photo in the lower-left corner. Your iPhone opens the Camera Roll (the album your iPhone uses to store the photos you take) and displays the photo. Tap Done when you're ready to return to the Camera app.

Working with Photos

Whether you add photos to your iPhone through an iTunes sync or by shooting new photos using the iPhone camera, after you've got images on your phone you can use the Photos app to work with those images. You can view the photos by album, event, face, or place; run a photo slide show; assign a photo to a contact; send a photo by email or text message; and delete any photos you don't need.

ⓖ *To learn how to use a photo as the iPhone wallpaper,* **see** *"Customizing the iPhone Wallpaper," p. 213.*

Viewing Photos

Your iPhone comes with a Photos app that enables you to view and work with the photos stored on your phone. The Photos app gives you four ways to view your photos:

- **By album:** If you have a Mac with iPhoto, you can create albums to store related photos. If you synced one or more albums from iTunes, you can view your photos by album in the Photos app. If you synced your photos by folder, instead, the Photos app creates an album for each folder and subfolder you synced.

- **By event:** If you have a Mac with iPhoto, your photos are organized by event. If you synced one or more events from iTunes, you can view your photos by event in the Photos app.

- **By face:** If you have a Mac with iPhoto 09 or later, you can identify the faces in your photos and then organize your photos by face. If you synced one or more faces from iTunes, you can view your photos by face in the Photos app.

- **By place:** If you have a Mac with iPhoto 09 or later, iPhoto can extract the location a photo was taken (assuming you took the photo with a GPS-equipped camera, such as your iPhone), or you can identify the places in your photos by hand, and iPhoto then organizes your photos by location. You can view your photos by place in the Photos app.

LET ME TRY IT

Viewing Photos by Album

1. In your iPhone's Home screen, tap Photos. The Photos app appears.

2. In the menu bar at the bottom of the screen, tap Albums.

3. Tap the album you want to view. The Photos app displays thumbnail versions of the album photos.

4. Tap the first photo you want to view. The Photos app displays the photo.

5. To view the next photo, either flick the screen to the left or tap the screen to reveal the controls (see Figure 10.4), and then tap the right arrow.

Figure 10.4 *Tap the screen to reveal the controls, and then tap the right and left arrows to navigate the photos.*

6. To view the previous photo, either flick the screen to the right or tap the screen to reveal the controls, and then tap the left arrow.

7. To select a different album, tap the screen to reveal the controls, tap the album name in the upper-left corner, tap Albums, and then tap the album you want to view.

 **LET ME TRY IT**

Viewing Photos by Event

1. In your iPhone's Home screen, tap Photos. The Photos app appears.

2. In the menu bar at the bottom of the screen, tap Events.

> If you didn't sync any events to your iPhone, you won't see the Events item in the menu bar.

3. Tap the event you want to view. The Photos app displays thumbnail versions of the event photos.

4. Tap the first photo you want to view. The Photos app displays the photo.

5. To view the next photo, either flick the screen to the left or tap the screen to reveal the controls, and then tap the right arrow.

6. To view the previous photo, either flick the screen to the right or tap the screen to reveal the controls, and then tap the left arrow.

7. To select a different event, tap the screen to reveal the controls, tap the event name in the upper-left corner, tap Events, and then tap the event you want to view.

 **LET ME TRY IT**

Viewing Photos by Face

1. In your iPhone's Home screen, tap Photos. The Photos app appears.

2. In the menu bar at the bottom of the screen, tap Faces.

> If you didn't sync any faces to your iPhone, you won't see the Faces item in the menu bar.

3. Tap the name of the person you want to view. The Photos app displays thumbnail versions of the person's photos.

4. Tap the first photo you want to view. The Photos app displays the photo.

5. To view the next photo, either flick the screen to the left or tap the screen to reveal the controls, and then tap the right arrow.

6. To view the previous photo, either flick the screen to the right or tap the screen to reveal the controls, and then tap the left arrow.

7. To select a different person, tap the screen to reveal the controls, tap the person's name in the upper-left corner, tap Faces, and then tap the person you want to view.

 SHOW ME   Media 10.2—A Video About Viewing Photos by Location
Access this video file through your registered Web Edition at
my.safaribooksonline.com/9780132182805/media.

 **LET ME TRY IT**

Viewing Photos by Place

1. In your iPhone's Home screen, tap Photos. The Photos app appears.

2. In the menu bar at the bottom of the screen, tap Places. The Photos app displays a map with pushpins indicating the locations of some of your photos.

> If your photos don't include any location data, then you won't see the Places item in the menu bar.

3. Spread your fingers on the screen over the area that has the photos you want to view. The Photos app zooms in on the area and displays pushpins for each location with a photo in that area.

4. Tap the pushpin of the place you want to view. The Photos app displays a banner showing the number of photos for that place, as shown in Figure 10.5.

5. Tap the blue More icon in the banner. The Photos app displays thumbnail versions of the place's photos.

6. Tap the first photo you want to view. The Photos app displays the photo.

Figure 10.5 *Zoom in on the general area you want to view, and then tap a location's pushpin to display the number of photos in that place.*

7. To view the next photo, either flick the screen to the left or tap the screen to reveal the controls, and then tap the right arrow.

8. To view the previous photo, either flick the screen to the right or tap the screen to reveal the controls, and then tap the left arrow.

9. To select a different place, tap the screen to reveal the controls, tap the *X* Photos button in the upper-left corner (where *X* is the number of photos for the current place), tap Places, and then tap the place you want to view.

Running a Photo Slide Show

As you saw in the previous sections, you can navigate the photos in an album, an event, a face, or a place either by flicking left and left or by tapping the screen and then tapping the Next and Previous arrows. However, what happens if you're eating a meal, sewing, or performing some other activity where your hands aren't free? In such cases, you can get your iPhone to do the work for you by starting a slide show where the Photos app displays your photos automatically every three seconds.

Running a Photo Slide Show

1. In your iPhone's Home screen, tap Photos. The Photos app appears.

2. Open the album, event, face, or place with the photos you want to include in the slide show. The Photos app displays thumbnail versions of the photos.

3. Tap the first photo you want to view. The Photos app displays the photo.

4. Tap the screen to display the controls.

5. Tap the Play button. The Photos app starts the slide show.

To customize your slide show, return to the Home screen, tap Settings, and then tap Photos. Tap Play Each Slide For to set the number of seconds each photo appears; tap Transition to select a transition effect between photos; tap Repeat to On to run the slide show continuously; and tap Shuffle to On to display the photos randomly.

Assigning a Photo to a Contact

If you have a photo of someone in your Contacts list, you can assign the photo to that contact. This means that the next time the person calls you, your iPhone will display the person's photo.

SHOW ME   Media 10.3—A Video About Assigning a Photo to a Contact
Access this video file through your registered Web Edition at
my.safaribooksonline.com/9780132182805/media.

Assigning a Photo to a Contact

1. In your iPhone's Home screen, tap Photos. The Photos app appears.

2. Open the album, event, face, or place that contains the contact's photo. The Photos app displays thumbnail versions of the photos.

3. Tap the photo you want to use for your contact. The Photos app displays the photo.

4. Tap the screen to display the controls.

5. Tap the Actions icon in the lower-left corner of the screen. The Photos app displays a list of actions you can perform.

6. Tap Assign to Contact. Your iPhone opens the All Contacts list.

7. Tap the contact you want to use. The Photos app displays the Move and Scale screen.

8. Drag the photo to bring the portion of the photo you want to use into view.

9. Spread your fingers on the screen to zoom in on the portion of the photo you want to use.

10. Tap Set Photo. The Photos app assigns the photo to the contact.

Sending a Photo

If you have a photo you want to share with another person, your iPhone enables you to send that photo to the recipient either via email or via an MMS message. (MMS is short for Multimedia Messaging Service, which is a form of text messaging service that also enables you to send photos and other media.) If you have a MobileMe account with Apple, you can also send a photo to your MobileMe Gallery to share with anyone who has access to your Gallery.

 **LET ME TRY IT**

Sending a Photo via Email

1. In your iPhone's Home screen, tap Photos. The Photos app appears.

2. Open the album, event, face, or place that contains the photo you want to send. The Photos app displays thumbnail versions of the photos.

3. Tap the photo you want to send. The Photos app displays the photo.

4. Tap the screen to display the controls.

5. Tap the Actions icon in the lower-left corner of the screen. The Photos app displays a list of actions you can perform.

6. Tap Email Photo. Your iPhone creates a new email message and attaches the photo to the message.

7. Tap inside the To field, and then either type or select your recipient.

8. Tap inside the Subject field, and type your message subject.

9. Tap inside the message body, and type a message for your recipient.

10. Tap Send. Your iPhone sends the message.

 LET ME TRY IT

Sending a Photo via MMS

1. In your iPhone's Home screen, tap Photos. The Photos app appears.

2. Open the album, event, face, or place that contains the photo you want to send. The Photos app displays thumbnail versions of the photos.

3. Tap the photo you want to send. The Photos app displays the photo.

4. Tap the screen to display the controls.

5. Tap the Actions icon in the lower-left corner of the screen. The Photos app displays a list of actions you can perform.

6. Tap MMS. Your iPhone creates a new MMS message and attaches the photo to the message.

7. Tap inside the To field, and then either type or select your recipient.

8. Tap inside the message body, and then type a message for your recipient.

9. Tap Send. Your iPhone sends the message.

 LET ME TRY IT

Sending a Photo to Your MobileMe Account

1. In your iPhone's Home screen, tap Photos. The Photos app appears.

2. Open the album, event, face, or place that contains the photo you want to send. The Photos app displays thumbnail versions of the photos.

3. Tap the photo you want to send. The Photos app displays the photo.

4. Tap the screen to display the controls.

5. Tap the Actions icon in the lower-left corner of the screen. The Photos app displays a list of actions you can perform.

6. Tap Send to MobileMe. Your iPhone displays the Publish Photo screen.

7. (Optional) Tap inside the Title field, and then type a title for the photo.

8. (Optional) Tap inside the Description field, and then type a description for the photo.

9. Scroll down to display your MobileMe Gallery albums, and then tap the album you want to use to store the photo.

10. Tap Publish. Your iPhone sends the photo to MobileMe and then displays the Photo Published dialog.

11. If you want to view the photo in your MobileMe Gallery, tap View on MobileMe. If you want to send an email message to tell someone you've published the photo, tap Tell a Friend. Otherwise, tap Close to return to the Photos app.

Deleting a Photo

If you took a photo with your iPhone's camera and you no longer need that photo or you don't like the photo, you should delete it to make the Camera Roll album easier to navigate and to save disk space on your iPhone.

> You can only delete photos from the Camera Roll. You can't delete photos from any other album, event, face, or place.

 LET ME TRY IT

Deleting a Photo

1. In your iPhone's Home screen, tap Photos. The Photos app appears.

2. Tap Albums. The Photos app displays a list of your albums.

3. Tap Camera Roll. The Photos app displays thumbnail versions of the photos in the Camera Roll album.

4. Tap the photo you want to delete. The Photos app displays the photo.

5. Tap the screen to display the controls.

6. Tap the Delete icon (the trash can in the lower-right corner of the screen). The Photos app asks you to confirm the deletion.

7. Tap Delete Photo. The Photos app removes the photo from the Camera Roll.

This chapter takes you through your iPhone's video features, including how to record and edit videos right on your iPhone, as well as how to play and share videos.

11

Recording and Playing Videos

Your iPhone's built-in camera takes decent photos, as you learned in Chapter 10, "Taking and Viewing Photos," but it also doubles as an effective and easy-to-use video camera. If you have an iPhone 4, you can actually record high-definition videos right on your phone. Even better, your iPhone's Camera app comes with built-in editing tools that you can use to trim unwanted footage.

The videos you take are stored on your iPhone, and you can later synchronize them to your computer. You can also synchronize your computer's videos to your iPhone. With your phone stocked with videos, you can then play the videos and share them with friends, family, and even total strangers on YouTube.

Synchronizing Videos

You see later in this chapter that you can use your iPhone's built-in camera (or cameras) to take videos right on your iPhone. However, if you've already got some videos on your computer, you can use iTunes to synchronize your computer videos to your iPhone. Conversely, you can also synchronize your iPhone's videos to your computer.

 LET ME TRY IT

Synchronizing Videos from Computer to iPhone

1. Connect your iPhone to your Mac or Windows PC.

2. In the iTunes sidebar, click your iPhone in the Devices branch. iTunes displays the Summary tab.

3. Click the Photos tab.

4. Activate the Sync Photos From check box.

5. Configure your photo syncing options, as described in Chapter 10.

🔘 *To learn how to set up photos syncing, **see** "Synchronizing Photos from Computer to iPhone," p. 159.*

6. Activate the Include Videos check box, as shown in Figure 11.1.

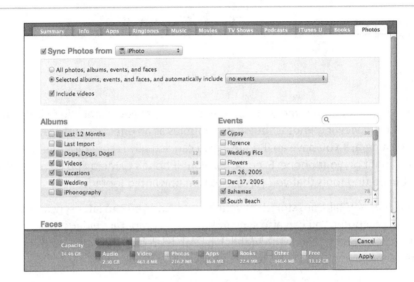

Figure 11.1   *To configure iTunes to sync videos to your iPhone, activate the Include Videos check box.*

7. Click Apply. iTunes synchronizes your computer's videos to your iPhone.

8. When the sync is complete, click the Eject icon next to your iPhone's name in the iTunes Devices list.

 **LET ME TRY IT**

Synchronizing Videos from iPhone to Mac

1. Connect your iPhone to your Mac. The iPhoto application appears.

2. In the iPhoto sidebar, click your iPhone in the Devices branch. iPhoto displays thumbnail versions of the phone's videos.

3. Use the Event Name text box to type a word or short phrase that describes the videos you're importing.

4. Hold down the Command key and click each video you want to import, as shown in Figure 11.2.

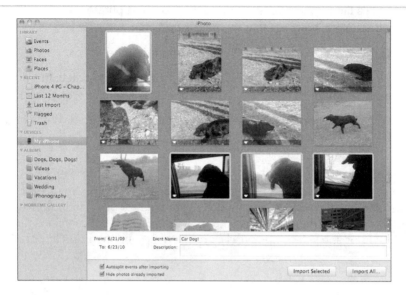

Figure 11.2   *On your Mac, you can use iPhoto to import the videos you've taken with your iPhone.*

As you can see in Figure 11.2, iPhoto denotes videos by displaying a small Camcorder icon in the lower-left corner of the thumbnail.

5.   Click Import Selected. iPhoto begins importing the videos. When the import is complete, iPhoto asks whether you want to delete the imported "photos" from your iPhone.

6.   If you no longer need to view the videos on your iPhone, click Delete Photos. Otherwise, if you still want the videos on your iPhone, click Keep Photos.

7.   In iTunes, click the Eject icon next to your iPhone's name in the Devices list.

 **LET ME TRY IT**

Synchronizing Videos from iPhone to Windows

1.   Connect your iPhone to your Windows PC. After a few moments, the AutoPlay window appears.

2.   Click Import Pictures and Videos. Windows displays the Import Pictures and Videos dialog box.

3. Type a tag for the videos. A *tag* is a word or short phrase that describes the videos. Note, however, that this step is optional.

4. Click Import. Your Windows PC begins importing the videos.

5. While the import is in progress, if you want Windows to delete the videos after the import is complete, activate the Erase After Importing check box.

6. When the import is complete, disconnect your iPhone from your Windows PC.

> If you've installed Windows Live Photo Gallery on your PC, you can use it to import photos from your iPhone. Connect your phone, open Windows Live Photo Gallery, and then select File, Import From a Camera or Scanner. In the Import Photos and Video window, click your iPhone, and then click Import.

Recording Videos with the iPhone Camera

If you have an iPhone 4, the main camera on the back of the phone can record high-definition (HD) video, and it also includes a built-in LED flash for recording low-light or dark scenes. The iPhone 4 also comes with a camera on the front, which is useful for taking videos of yourself. Also, the latest iPhone software comes with a tap-to-focus feature.

TELL ME MORE Media 11.1—Recording HD Video with Your iPhone

To listen to a free audio recording about recording HD videos with your iPhone, log on to my.safaribooksonline.com/9780132182805/media.

 **LET ME TRY IT**

Recording a Video with the iPhone Camera

1. In the iPhone Home screen, tap the Camera icon to open the Camera app.

2. Tap the mode switch in the lower-right corner from Camera to Video, as shown in Figure 11.3.

Figure 11.3 *To record video with your iPhone, first tap the mode switch to change the setting from Camera to Video.*

3. (iPhone 4) To choose an LED flash setting, tap the Flash icon in the upper-left corner of the screen; then tap No (to ensure the flash doesn't come on during the recording), Yes (to ensure the flash always stays on during the recording), or Auto (to let your iPhone determine whether the flash is required).

4. To focus the image, tap the screen on the spot you want in focus.

5. (iPhone 4) To switch to the front camera, tap the Switch Cameras icon, located in the upper-right corner of the screen.

6. Tap the Record button in the center of the Camera app toolbar. Your iPhone begins recording the video.

7. When you've finished your recording, tap the Record button again. Your iPhone saves the video and then displays a thumbnail version of the video in the lower-left corner.

If you want to watch the video you just recorded, tap the thumbnail of the video in the lower-left corner. Your iPhone opens the Camera Roll (the album your iPhone uses to store the videos you record) and displays the video's opening frame. Tap Play to start the video. Tap Done when you're ready to return to the Camera app.

Editing iPhone Videos

When you record a video on your iPhone, you might end up with unneeded footage at the beginning or the end of the video (or both). Normally, you'd fix this by syncing the video to your computer, using an application such as iMovie to edit the video, and then syncing the video back to your iPhone. Fortunately, your iPhone's Camera app gives you a much easier method for doing this. That is, the Camera app enables you to trim unneeded scenes from the beginning and the end of the video, right on your iPhone.

 SHOW ME   **Media 11.2—A Video About Editing iPhone Videos**
Access this video file through your registered Web Edition at
my.safaribooksonline.com/9780132182805/media.

 LET ME TRY IT

Editing an iPhone Video

1. In the iPhone Home screen, tap Photos. The Photos app appears.

2. Tap Albums. The Photos app opens the Albums screen.

3. Tap Camera Roll. The Photos app opens the Camera Roll album and displays thumbnail versions of your photos and videos.

4. Tap the video you want to edit. (Remember that the Photos app denotes videos by displaying a small Camcorder icon in the lower-left corner of the thumbnail.)

5. Tap the screen to display the controls, which include a timeline of the video at the top of the screen.

6. Tap and drag the left edge of the timeline to set the starting point of the video.

7. Tap and drag the right edge of the timeline to set the ending point of the video. The trimmed timeline appears surrounded by orange, as shown in Figure 11.4.

Figure 11.4 *Tap and drag the left and right edges of the timeline to trim scenes from the beginning and end of the video, respectively.*

8. Tap Trim.

9. If you want to apply the trim to the original video file, tap Trim Original. Otherwise, tap Save as New Clip to keep the original and save the trimmed version as a new video. The Photos app trims the video.

Working with Videos on Your iPhone

Whether you populate your iPhone with videos through an iTunes sync or by recording new videos using the iPhone camera, after you've got videos on your phone you can use the Photos app to work with those videos. You can play the videos, send a video by email or text message, upload a video to MobileMe or YouTube, and delete any videos you don't need.

Playing a Video

The Photos app enables you to view and work with the videos stored on your iPhone. Although all the videos you record using your iPhone are stored in the Camera Roll album, the videos you sync from iTunes can appear in different albums, events, faces, and places.

 For the details on viewing videos by album, event, face, or place, **see** "Viewing Photos," p. 164.

 LET ME TRY IT

Playing a Video

1. In your iPhone's Home screen, tap Photos. The Photos app appears.

2. In the menu bar at the bottom of the screen, tap the category where your video appears: Albums, Events, Faces, or Places.

3. Tap the album, event, face, or place you want to view. The Photos app displays thumbnail versions of the photos and videos. (Remember that the Photos app denotes videos by displaying a small Camcorder icon in the lower-left corner of the thumbnail.)

4. Tap the video you want to watch. The Photos app displays the first frame of the video.

5. Tap Play. The Photos app begins playing the video.

6. To pause the playback, tap the screen to reveal the controls, as shown in Figure 11.5, and then tap Pause. To resume playback, tap the screen and then tap Play.

Sending a Video

If you have a video you want to share with another person, your iPhone enables you to send that video to the recipient either via email or via an MMS (Multimedia Messaging Service) message. If you have a MobileMe account with Apple, you can also send a video to your MobileMe Gallery to share with anyone who has access to your Gallery. In addition, if you have a YouTube account, you can upload your video to YouTube.

Figure 11.5   *Tap the screen to reveal the controls, and then tap the Pause button to temporarily stop the playback.*

 **LET ME TRY IT**

Sending a Video via Email

1. In your iPhone's Home screen, tap Photos. The Photos app appears.

2. Open the album, event, face, or place that contains the video you want to send. The Photos app displays thumbnail versions of the photos and videos.

3. Tap the video you want to send. The Photos app displays the video.

4. Tap the screen to display the controls.

5. Tap the Actions icon in the lower-left corner of the screen. The Photos app displays a list of actions you can perform.

6. Tap Email Video. Your iPhone creates a new email message and attaches the video to the message.

> If your video is too big to send via email, the Photos app displays a dialog box to let you know. In that case, tap OK, trim the video as described earlier, and then tap Email.

7. Tap inside the To field, and then either type or select your recipient.

8. Tap inside the Subject field, and type your message subject.

9. Tap inside the message body, and type a message for your recipient.

10. Tap Send. Your iPhone sends the message.

 LET ME TRY IT

Sending a Video via MMS

1. In your iPhone's Home screen, tap Photos. The Photos app appears.

2. Open the album, event, face, or place that contains the video you want to send. The Photos app displays thumbnail versions of the photos and videos.

3. Tap the video you want to send. The Photos app displays the video.

4. Tap the screen to display the controls.

5. Tap the Actions icon in the lower-left corner of the screen. The Photos app displays a list of actions you can perform.

6. Tap MMS. Your iPhone creates a new MMS message and attaches the video to the message.

> If your video is too big to send via MMS, the Photos app displays a dialog box to let you know. In that case, tap OK, trim the video as described earlier, and then tap MMS.

7. Tap inside the To field, and then either type or select your recipient.

8. Tap inside the message body, and type a message for your recipient.

9. Tap Send. Your iPhone sends the message.

LET ME TRY IT

Sending a Video to Your MobileMe Account

1. In your iPhone's Home screen, tap Photos. The Photos app appears.

2. Open the album, event, face, or place that contains the video you want to send. The Photos app displays thumbnail versions of the photos and videos.

3. Tap the video you want to send. The Photos app displays the video.

4. Tap the screen to display the controls.

5. Tap the Actions icon in the lower-left corner of the screen. The Photos app displays a list of actions you can perform.

6. Tap Send to MobileMe. Your iPhone displays the Publish Video screen.

7. (Optional) Tap inside the Title field, and then type a title for the video.

8. (Optional) Tap inside the Description field, and then type a description for the video.

9. Scroll down to display your MobileMe Gallery albums, and then tap the album you want to use to store the video.

10. Tap Publish. Your iPhone sends the video to MobileMe and then displays the Published dialog.

11. If you want to view the video in your MobileMe Gallery, tap View on MobileMe. If you want to send an email message to tell someone you've pub-lished the video, tap Tell a Friend. Otherwise, tap Close to return to the Pho-tos app.

SHOW ME   Media 11.3—A Video About Publishing a Video to YouTube
Access this video file through your registered Web Edition at my.safaribooksonline.com/9780132182805/media.

LET ME TRY IT

Sending a Video to YouTube

1. In your iPhone's Home screen, tap Photos. The Photos app appears.

2. Open the album, event, face, or place that contains the video you want to send. The Photos app displays thumbnail versions of the photos and videos.

3. Tap the video you want to send. The Photos app displays the video.

4. Tap the screen to display the controls.

5. Tap the Actions icon in the lower-left corner of the screen. The Photos app displays a list of actions you can perform.

6. Tap Send to YouTube. If this is the first time you have sent a video to YouTube, the Photos app prompts you to log on to your YouTube account.

7. Enter your YouTube username and password. The Photos app displays the Publish Video screen.

8. Tap inside the Title field, and then type a title for the video.

9. Tap inside the Description field, and then type a description for the video.

10. Tap inside the Tag field, and then type a tag for the video.

11. Tap Category, and then tap the YouTube category that applies to your video.

12. Tap Publish. Your iPhone sends the video to YouTube and then displays the Published dialog.

13. If you want to view the video on YouTube, tap View on YouTube. If you want to send an email message to tell someone you've published the video, tap Tell a Friend. Otherwise, tap Close to return to the Photos app.

Deleting a Video

If you recorded a video with your iPhone's camera and you no longer need that video or you don't like the video, you should delete it to make the Camera Roll album easier to navigate and to save disk space on your iPhone.

You can only delete videos from the Camera Roll. You can't delete videos from any other album, event, face, or place.

Deleting a Video

1. In your iPhone's Home screen, tap Photos. The Photos app appears.

2. Tap Albums. The Photos app displays a list of your albums.

3. Tap Camera Roll. The Photos app displays thumbnail versions of the photos and videos in the Camera Roll album.

4. Tap the video you want to delete. The Photos app displays the video.

5. Tap the screen to display the controls.

6. Tap the Delete icon (the trash can in the lower-right corner of the screen). The Photos app asks you to confirm the deletion.

7. Tap Delete Video. The Photos app removes the video from the Camera Roll.

This chapter introduces you to the other apps
that come with your iPhone, including Messages,
Calculator, Compass, and the App Store.

12

Working with Apps and the App Store

So far in this book you've looked at all the major apps that come preloaded with your iPhone: Settings, Phone, Safari, Mail, iPod, iTunes, Contacts, Calendar, Clock, Maps, Camera, and Photos. However, your iPhone comes populated with quite a few other apps that enable you to send text messages, perform calculations, take notes, view weather forecasts, watch YouTube videos, and more. Your iPhone also comes with an app called App Store that enables you to add even more apps to your phone. This chapter shows you how to use these apps and also tells you about the app multitasking capabilities built in to your iPhone.

Getting to Know the Rest of the iPhone Apps

Although you'll probably spend most of your iPhone time using the major apps that you learned about in the first 11 chapters of this book, the remaining apps have their uses, too. The next few sections take you through 9 of the remaining 10 apps (the 10th, App Store, comes a bit later in the chapter): Messages, Calculator, Compass, Notes, Stocks, Voice Memos, Weather, YouTube, and Game Center.

Sending Text Messages

You use the Messages app to exchange text messages with another person. Text messages are sent and received using the Short Message Service (SMS), with *short* being the operative word here: SMS messages can't be any longer than 160 characters. Note, as well, that text messages are cell phone–to–cell phone messages, meaning that you can only send a text message to another cell phone number. Your iPhone also supports Multimedia Messaging Service (MMS), which you can use to send maps, photos, videos, and more.

To learn how to use MMS to send a photo, **see** "Sending a Photo via MMS," p. 171.

ⓖ *To learn how to use MMS to send a video,* ***see*** *"Sending a Video via MMS," p. 182.*

If someone sends you a text message, your iPhone displays the message in a notification dialog like the one shown in Figure 12.1. It also adds 1 to the Messages app icon in the Home screen (again, see Figure 12.1). To continue the conversation, tap Reply. If you can't text right now, tap Close, instead, and you can reply later when it's convenient.

Figure 12.1   *When you receive a text, your iPhone displays a notification like the one shown here.*

You can also initiate your own text message conversations, as described next.

 **LET ME TRY IT**

Sending Text Messages

1. Tap the Messages icon in the iPhone Home screen. The Messages screen appears.

2. Tap the New Message icon in the upper-right corner of the screen. Your iPhone displays the New Message screen.

3. Use the To field to type the cell phone of the person you want to text with. If you already have that person's cell number in your Contacts list, tap the blue Add (+) icon to display your contacts, tap the contact, and then tap the cell phone number.

4. Tap inside the text box that appears to the left of the Send button, and then type your message. Figure 12.2 shows an example.

Figure 12.2 *Type the cell number or select the contact, and then use the text box to type your message.*

5. Tap Send. The Messages app sends your message to the person's cell phone.

6. When the person responds, read the message and then repeat steps 4 and 5 to continue the conversation.

Calculating with Calculator

If you need to make some quick calculations—such as checking your grocery bill or calculating a restaurant tip—your iPhone comes with a Calculator app that, when your iPhone is in portrait mode, looks just like a basic calculator (see Figure 12.3). It has a numeric keypad; buttons for addition (+), subtraction (–), multiplication (×), and division (÷); and the standard calculator memory buttons.

Figure 12.3   *In portrait mode, the Calculator app looks just like a basic calculator.*

However, if you rotate your iPhone into landscape mode, the Calculator app changes to the configuration shown in Figure 12.4. You still see the standard calculator buttons on the right, but on the left you now see buttons for more sophisticated operations such as squares, cubes, square roots, factorials, logarithms, trigonometric functions, and much more.

Figure 12.4   *In landscape mode, the Calculator app sprouts many sophisticated mathematical features, such as square roots, logarithms, and trigonometric functions.*

To open the Calculator app, tap the Utilities folder to open the folder, and then tap the Calculator icon.

Using the Compass to Learn Which Way You're Facing

If you have an iPhone 4 or an iPhone 3GS, your phone comes with a built-in magnetometer, which is an instrument that measures the direction and strength of the magnetic field that surrounds the phone. Assuming there isn't some intense magnetic field nearby, the magnetometer measures the direction of the earth's magnetic field, which means it always knows which way is north.

So, you might therefore assume you can use your iPhone as a compass. You can't do that directly, but you can do it using the Compass app. To open the Compass app, tap the Utilities folder to open the folder and then tap the Compass icon. Figure 12.5 shows the compass app. The red arrow marked N (for north) always points north, and the direction that appears above the compass tells you which direction you're currently facing.

Figure 12.5 *The Compass app tells you which way you're facing.*

Taking Notes

What do you do if you're running around town and you suddenly think of a great line for an upcoming speech, come up with a couple of good ideas for a project you're working on, or figure out the solution to some problem that's been rattling around in your head? You might be tempted to pull out a piece of paper and a pen and scribble a note to yourself, but you can use your iPhone's Notes app to type a note directly into your phone. You can then email the note to yourself.

 **LET ME TRY IT**

Writing a Note

1. In the Home screen, tap the Utilities folder. Your iPhone opens the Utilities folder.

2. Tap Notes. Your iPhone opens the Notes app.

3. Tap the Add (+) icon at the upper-right corner of the screen. The New Note screen appears.

4. Type your note.

5. Tap Done. The Notes app displays the note, as shown in Figure 12.6.

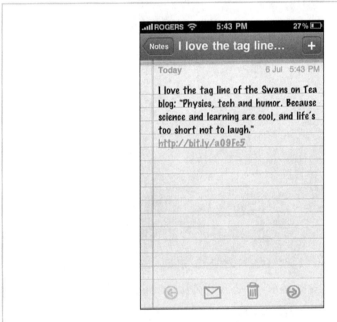

Figure 12.6   *A completed note.*

6. To email the note, tap the Envelope icon in the menu bar to create a new email message that includes the note text, add a recipient, and then tap Send.

Tracking Your Stocks

You can view the rise and fall of particular stocks throughout the day with your iPhone's Stocks app. The stock data isn't real time—there's a 20-minute lag time—but that's standard for these kinds of free stock information services. You can track your own portfolio of stocks or stock indexes, and for each one you see the current price, how much the stock is up or down today, and a graph that shows the stock's price movements over the past year.

 **LET ME TRY IT**

Adding a Stock to the Stocks App

1. In the Home screen, tap the Utilities folder. Your iPhone opens the Utilities folder.

2. Tap Stocks. Your iPhone opens the Stocks app.

3. Tap the *i* icon in the lower-right corner to open the Stocks screen.

4. Tap the Add (+) icon. The Add Stock screen opens and the keyboard appears.

5. Type the company or index name or its abbreviation (if you know it).

6. Tap Search. A list of matching companies or indexes appears.

7. Tap the company or index that you want. The stock is added to your list and you end up back on the Stocks screen.

8. Tap % (if you want to see the percentage the stock has changed today), Price (if you want to see how much the stock has changed today), or Mkt Cap (if you want to see how the company's market capitalization has changed today).

9. Tap Done. The Stocks app displays the data for the company or index you added, as shown in Figure 12.7.

Recording Voice Memos

Your iPhone's Notes app, which you learned about in the previous section, is handy if you have the time to tap out your note, but when inspiration (or whatever) strikes, you might need to get your thoughts in some sort of concrete form in a hurry. Similarly, the Notes app isn't very useful if you're driving or otherwise have your hands occupied.

Figure 12.7 *You can add stocks or stock indexes to the Stocks app and track prices, percentage changes, or market capitalization over a range from one day to two years.*

If you need to record a thought in a hurry, or if it's not convenient for you to type right now, you can still preserve your thoughts using the Voice Memos app, which records your voice. You can also use Voice Memos to record lectures, interviews, meetings, or podcasts.

 SHOW ME   **Media 12.1—A Video About Recording and Trimming a Voice Memo**
Access this video file through your registered Web Edition at my.safaribooksonline.com/9780132182805/media.

 **LET ME TRY IT**

Recording a Voice Memo

1. In the Home screen, tap the Utilities folder. Your iPhone opens the Utilities folder.

2. Tap Voice Memos. Your iPhone opens the Voice Memos app, shown in Figure 12.8.

Figure 12.8   *Use the Voice Memos app to record your thoughts, ideas, memos, interviews, or podcasts.*

3. As a test, speak into the microphone and watch the VU (volume unit) meter. If the needle spikes into the red zone, you need to speak a bit quieter to avoid distortion.

4. Tap the red Record button. iPhone sounds a ding and displays "Recording" below the status bar, along with the running length of the recording.

5. Speak into the iPhone to record your memo. If you need to pause the recording, tap the red Pause button; when you're ready to resume, tap the red Record button.

6. When you've finished, tap the black Stop button.

7. Tap the Voice Memos button to the right of the VU meter. The Voice Memos screen appears, and your memo starts playing back. (To hear it through the iPhone, tap the Speaker icon.)

8. Tap the voice memo and then tap the blue More Info button. Voice Memos displays the Info window for the recording, as shown in Figure 12.9.

9. Tap the recording. The Label screen appears.

10. Tap the label you want to assign to the recording, and then tap Info.

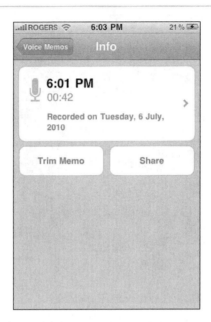

Figure 12.9 *Use the Info screen to label, trim, and share the recording.*

11. If the memo is too long or contains dead air either at the beginning or end, tap Trim Memo. The Trim Memo screen appears.

12. Tap and drag the handles on the left and right ends of the memo timeline to set the start and end points of the memo.

13. Tap Trim Voice Memo. Voice Memos trims the recording and returns you to the Info screen.

Getting the Weather Forecast

If you're getting ready for a trip to another city, it's a good idea to check the current weather in that city. Why? Because if the weather in that city is radically different from your present weather, you need to decide what's best to wear while traveling. You should also check the forecast for the other city because that helps you decide which clothes to pack.

It's normally a bit of a hassle to locate not only the current weather for a city, but also its weather forecast. Not so with your iPhone, which comes with a Weather app that's quick and easy to use. You can add multiple cities, and for each city you see not only the current conditions, but also the six-day forecast.

SHOW ME   Media 12.2—A Video About Adding a Weather Forecast
Access this video file through your registered Web Edition at
my.safaribooksonline.com/9780132182805/media.

 **LET ME TRY IT**

Getting the Weather Forecast for a City

1. In the Home screen, tap Weather. Your iPhone opens the Weather app.

2. Tap the *i* icon in the lower-right corner of the screen. This opens the Weather screen.

3. Tap the Add (+) icon in the upper-left corner of the screen. The Weather app prompts you to enter a city, state, or ZIP code.

4. Type the city. If you know a ZIP or postal code in the city, you can type that instead.

5. Tap Search to see a list of matching cities.

6. Tap the city that you want. Your iPhone returns you to the Weather screen.

7. Tap either Celsius or Fahrenheit.

8. Tap Done. Your iPhone displays the current conditions and the forecast for the city you added, as shown in Figure 12.10.

> If the forecast shows a blue background, it means that it's currently daytime in the city. If you see a purple background, instead, it's currently nighttime in the city.

Watching YouTube Videos

Your iPhone comes with a YouTube app right in the Home screen, so you can watch whatever video everyone's talking about or just browse around for interesting finds.

YouTube videos tend to be in Flash, a video format that the iPhone doesn't recognize. However, many of YouTube's videos have been converted to a format called H.264, which is a much higher-quality video format and is playable on your iPhone. The YouTube app plays only these H.264 videos.

Figure 12.10   *The Weather app shows the current conditions and the six-day forecast for whatever city you choose.*

To fire up the YouTube app, press the Home button to return to the Home screen and then tap the YouTube icon.

YouTube's collection of talking cats, stupid human tricks, and TV snippets is vast, to say the least. To help you apply at least a bit of order to the YouTube chaos, your iPhone organizes the YouTube app in a similar way to the iPod feature. That is, you get four browse buttons in the menu bar (Featured, Most Viewed, Search, and Favorites) and a More button that, when tapped, tosses up six more browse buttons (Most Recent, Top Rated, History, My Video, Subscription, and Playlists).

Here's a summary of what each browse button does for you:

- **Featured:** Tap this button to display a list of videos picked by the YouTube editors. The list shows each video's name, star rating, popularity, and length.

- **Most Viewed:** Tap this to see the videos with the most views. At the top you can tap Today, This Week, and All. This chooses the top-viewed videos of today, this week, or of all time. At the bottom of the list, you can tap Load More, which loads 25 more Most Viewed videos.

- **Search:** Tap this to display a Search text box. Tap inside the box, enter a search phrase, and then tap Search. YouTube sends back a list of videos that match your search term.

- **Favorites:** Tap this button to see a list of videos that you've bookmarked as being favorites.

- **Most Recent:** Tap here to see the videos that have been posted on YouTube most recently.

- **Top Rated:** Tap this button to display the videos that have the highest user ratings.

- **History:** Give this a tap to see the videos that you've viewed.

- **My Videos:** Tap this button to log on to YouTube and see a list of the videos you've uploaded.

- **Subscriptions:** Tap this button to log on to YouTube and see a list of your video subscriptions.

- **Playlists:** Tap this button to log on to YouTube and see the video playlists you've created.

 **LET ME TRY IT**

Watching a YouTube Video

1. In the Home screen, tap YouTube to open the YouTube app.

2. Use the browse buttons to display a list of videos.

3. Tap the video you want to view. The YouTube app opens the video and starts playing it.

4. Tap the screen. The YouTube app reveals the playback controls, as shown in Figure 12.11.

5. Tap Pause to temporarily suspend the video; Tap Play to resume the video.

6. To fast forward or rewind the video, tap and drag the playback slider at the top of the screen.

7. To end the playback, tap Done.

Playing with Game Center

Game Center is a social network for mobile gaming. You can make friends with other gamers, participate in multiplayer games, earn achievements, and more. As this book was going to press, Apple had announced that the Game Center network would become available later in 2010, so it might be up and running by the time

Figure 12.11   *During video playback, tap the screen to see the controls.*

you read this. To get ready for Game Center, you need to set up your Game Center account and then learn how to send and accept friend requests.

 **LET ME TRY IT**

Setting Up Your Game Center Account

1. In the Home screen, tap the Game Center icon to launch Game Center. The first time you run Game Center, your iPhone asks whether you want to allow the app to send you push notifications.

2. Tap OK. The Welcome to Game Center screen appears.

3. Type your iTunes Store account address (if it's not already filled in for you, which it should be).

4. Type your iTunes Store password.

5. Tap Sign In. The Game Center Terms and Conditions screen appears.

6. Tap Agree. Game Center asks you to confirm.

7. Tap Agree. The New Account screen appears.

8. In the Nickname field, type the nickname you want to use to identify yourself on Game Center.

9. Tap Next. Game Center creates your account and displays the Me screen, which is your Game Center home base.

LET ME TRY IT

Send a Friend Request

1. In Game Center, tap Friends.
2. Tap the Add (+) icon. The Friend Request screen appears.
3. Use the To field to enter your friend's email address or Game Center nickname.
4. Tap Send. Game Center sends the requests and displays a message telling you you'll only see the friend in your Friends list if he or she accepts your invitation.
5. Tap OK.

 LET ME TRY IT

Accept a Friend Request

1. In Game Center, tap Requests. Game Center displays a list of your pending friend requests, as shown in Figure 12.12.

Figure 12.12   *Tap Requests to see a list of your pending friend requests.*

2. Tap the request you want to accept. Game Center displays a screen for the user making the request.
3. Tap Accept. Game Center adds the user to your Friends list.

Multitasking Apps

If you have an iPhone 4 or an iPhone 3GS, you can run multiple apps at the same time. This is useful if, say, you're playing a game and a text message comes in because you can switch to the message to read and possibly respond to it and then switch back to your game and resume where you left off.

Whenever you run an app and then switch to another app, your iPhone keeps the first app running in the background. In most cases, the first app does nothing while it's in the background, it doesn't take any processor time away from your current app, and it doesn't use battery power. This means that you're free to open as many apps as you like. However, if the first app is performing some task and you switch to another app, the first app will continue to perform the task in the background.

TELL ME MORE   Media 12.3—Understanding iPhone Multitasking

To listen to a free audio recording about iPhone multitasking, log on to my.safaribooksonline.com/9780132182805/media.

LET ME TRY IT

Multitasking Apps

1. Start all the apps you want to use.

2. Double-press the Home button. Your iPhone displays a list of running apps, as shown in Figure 12.13.

3. If needed, flick the list (found on the bottom) left or right to bring the app you want to use into view.

4. Tap the app you want to use. Your iPhone switches to the app and leaves the previous app running in the background.

To make the list of running apps easier to navigate, you should shut down any apps you won't be using for a while. Double-press the Home button to display the running app list, press and hold any app to put the icons into edit mode, and then tap the X on any app you want to shut down. When you've finished, press the Home button to exit edit mode.

Figure 12.13 *On your iPhone 4 or 3GS, double-press the Home button to display the list of running apps.*

Extending Your iPhone with the App Store

Your iPhone comes stocked with 22 apps that enable you to do a wide variety of tasks, from surfing the Web to tracking contacts and appointments to capturing photos and videos. You can do a lot with the default iPhone apps, but you can't do everything. For example, you can't read eBooks, learn a foreign language, or get the name of the song that's currently playing on the radio.

Fortunately, you can extend your iPhone to perform all of these tasks and thousands more by downloading apps from the App Store. There are well over a hundred thousand apps to choose from, most of which are either free or cost just a few dollars.

To open the App Store on your iPhone, tap the App Store icon in the Home screen. Figure 12.14 shows the App Store screen.

The App Store interface is similar to the one you see in the iTunes Store, with five browse buttons in the menu bar:

- **Featured:** This button displays a list of apps picked by the App Store editors. The list shows each app's name, icon, star rating, number of reviews, and price. Tap New to see the latest apps, and tap What's Hot to see the most popular items.

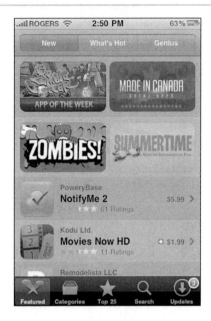

Figure 12.14 *In your iPhone's Home screen, tap the App Store icon to open the App Store.*

- **Categories:** Tap this button to see a list of app categories, such as Utilities and Social Networking. Tap a category to see a list of the apps available.

- **Top 25:** Tap this button to see a list of the 25 most often downloaded apps in three lists: Top Paid, Top Free, and Top Grossing.

- **Search:** Tap this button to display a Search text box. Tap inside the box, enter a search phrase, and then tap Search. App Store sends back a list of apps that match your search term.

- **Updates:** If you see a badge attached to this button (as shown in Figure 12.14), it means that one or more of the apps you've installed have updated versions available. Tap this button, and then tap an app to update it.

Note, too, that you can also access the App Store on your computer. Open iTunes, click iTunes Store, and then click App Store. Any applications you download to your computer can then be synced to your iPhone.

LET ME TRY IT

Installing an App

1. On the iPhone's Home screen, tap App Store. Your iPhone launches the App Store.

2. Use the App Store interface to locate the app you want to install.

3. Tap the app. The App Store displays information about the app, including user ratings and reviews, app info, screenshots, and more.

4. Tap the Price button. If the app is free, tap the Free button, instead.

5. Tap Buy Now. If the app is free, tap Install, instead. The App Store prompts you for your iTunes Store password.

6. Type your password and tap OK. Your iPhone downloads and installs the app.

 LET ME TRY IT

Syncing Apps

1. Connect your iPhone to your Mac or Windows PC.

2. In the iTunes sidebar, click your iPhone in the Devices branch. iTunes displays the Summary tab.

3. Click the Apps tab.

4. Activate the Sync Apps check box, as shown in Figure 12.15.

5. Activate the check box beside each app you want to synchronize with your iPhone.

6. Click Apply. iTunes synchronizes your computer's apps to your iPhone.

7. When the sync is complete, click the Eject icon next to your iPhone's name in the iTunes Devices list.

Figure 12.15   *Activate the Sync Apps check box, and then select the apps you want to sync.*

This chapter shows you various customization
tasks for the Home screen, sounds, wallpaper,
keyboard, and more.

13

Customizing Your iPhone

Your iPhone certainly works easily and intuitively right out of the box, but that
doesn't mean you can't make your iPhone even better. That's because we all have
unique ways of working and playing, so chances are your iPhone isn't configured
ideally for the way you use it. For example, the Home screen icons might not be
arranged optimally, or you might find that your iPhone is just too noisy for your
tastes.

Fortunately, the iPhone comes with a wide array of customization tools, settings,
and options, so you can almost always improve the way your iPhone works and
looks. This chapter takes you through 10 of the most useful iPhone customization
tweaks.

Customizing the Home Screen

The Home screen is one of your iPhone's most important features because you use
it to launch the apps that make your iPhone do useful and fun things. If you use
your iPhone a lot, you use the Home screen a lot, so it pays to take a bit of time to
customize the Home screen to suit the way you use your iPhone. This is particularly
true if you've been using the App Store to install many new apps, so you now have
multiple Home screens to navigate.

To learn how to use the App Store, **see** "Extending Your iPhone with the
App Store," p. 203.

To make your Home screen faster and more efficient, you can do two things:

- **Rearrange the Home screen icons:** This means that you move the apps you
  use most often to the Dock or the first or second Home screen, and you move
  the apps you use the least to the last Home screen.

- **Create Home screen app folders:** This means that you combine two or more
  similar apps in a special icon called an app folder. This reduces the overall
  number of icons on the Home screens, and it makes it easier for you to find
  similar apps because they're all together within the folder. You can create as
  many app folders as you need.

SHOW ME   Media 13.1—A Video About Rearranging Home Screen Icons

Access this video file through your registered Web Edition at my.safaribooksonline.com/9780132182805/media.

 LET ME TRY IT

Rearranging the Home Screen Icons

1. Tap and hold any Home screen icon. Your iPhone enters icon edit mode, which it indicates by setting the icons jiggling.

2. To move an icon to a different position in the current screen, tap and drag the icon to the position you want (make sure you position the icons between two existing icons), and then release the icon.

3. To move an icon to an earlier Home screen, tap and drag the icon to the left edge of the screen. Your iPhone displays the next screen to the left, you keep dragging until you get to the screen you want, and then you release the icon.

4. To move an icon to a later Home screen, tap and drag the icon to the right edge of the screen. Your iPhone displays the next screen to the right, you keep dragging until you get to the screen you want, and then you release the icon.

5. To move an icon onto the Dock, first tap and drag an existing Dock icon out of the Dock and onto the screen where you want it to appear. You can then drag the new icon into the Dock and drop it there.

6. When you are done, press the Home button. Your iPhone exits icon edit mode.

 **SHOW ME**   Media 13.2—A Video About Creating App Folders

Access this video file through your registered Web Edition at my.safaribooksonline.com/9780132182805/media.

 **LET ME TRY IT**

Creating Home Screen App Folders

1. Tap and hold any Home screen icon. Your iPhone enters icon edit mode, which it indicates by setting the icons jiggling.

2. Tap and drag an icon on top of another icon that you want to include in the same folder, and then release the icon. Your iPhone creates the app folder, adds the two icons to it, and then displays a text box with a suggested name for the folder, as shown in Figure 13.1.

Figure 13.1   *When you drop one app on top of a similar app, your iPhone suggests a folder name based on the category used by both apps.*

3. Edit the app folder name, if desired.

4. Tap the screen above the folder name. Your iPhone closes the folder.

5. To add another app to the folder, drag the app's icon and drop it on the folder. Repeat for any other apps you want to add to the folder.

You can add a maximum of 12 app icons to each app folder.

6. When you have finished, press the Home button. Your iPhone exits icon edit mode.

Putting the iPhone in Airplane Mode

Your iPhone comes with built-in antennas that are constantly on the lookout for three different kinds of wireless signals: cellular, Wi-Fi, and Bluetooth. These antennas are very useful in most situations, but they can cause problems when you're on an airplane because they can interfere with the aircraft's onboard systems. To prevent that, you can place your iPhone into *airplane mode*, which disables all three antennas.

Airplane mode is also useful if you're running low on your iPhone battery and there's no power outlet near you. The constant probing of the antennas for nearby wireless signals is also a constant drain on the battery, so if you don't need any wireless connections for a while, switch to airplane mode to preserve battery life.

 **LET ME TRY IT**

Putting the iPhone in Airplane Mode

1. In the Home screen, tap Settings. Your iPhone opens the Settings app.

2. Tap the Airplane Mode switch to On, as shown in Figure 13.2. Your iPhone disables the antennas and displays an airplane icon on the left side of the status bar, as shown in Figure 13.2.

Customizing the iPhone's Sounds

Your iPhone uses sounds to give you aural feedback on what's currently happening on the phone. The iPhone rings when a call comes in, of course, but you also hear sounds when you receive a new text message, a new voicemail, or a new email message. Your iPhone also plays a sound when you send an email message and when a calendar event alert appears. Finally, your iPhone also plays a sound when you lock and unlock the phone and when you tap keys on the virtual keyboard. You can control these sounds either by selecting different sounds to play for incoming phone calls and text messages or by toggling individual sounds on and off.

Airplane Mode icon

Figure 13.2   *When you tap the Airplane Mode switch to On, your iPhone reminds you by adding an airplane icon to the status bar.*

LET ME TRY IT

Customizing the iPhone's Sounds

1. In the Home screen, tap Settings to launch the Settings app.

2. Tap Sounds. The Sounds screen appears, as shown in Figure 13.3.

3. In the Silent section, leave the Vibrate switch set to On to have your iPhone vibrate when the phone is in silent mode (that is, when you have flicked the Ring/Silent switch to the Silent position).

To learn how to put your iPhone into silent mode, **see** "Working with the Ring/Silent Switch," p. 9.

4. In the Ring section, leave the Vibrate switch set to On to have your iPhone vibrate when the phone is in ring mode.

5. Drag the volume slider to set the volume of the ringtone that plays when a call comes in.

Figure 13.3   *Open the Settings app and then tap Sounds to see your iPhone's Sounds settings.*

6. To set a different default ringtone, tap Ringtone to open the Ringtone screen, tap the ringtone you want to use (your iPhone plays a preview), and then tap Sounds to return to the Sounds screen.

7. To set a different incoming text message sound, tap New Text Message to open the New Text Message screen, tap the sound effect you want to use (your iPhone plays a preview), and then tap Sounds to return to the Sounds screen.

8. For each of the remaining settings—New Voicemail, New Mail, Sent Mail, Calendar Alerts, Lock Sounds, and Keyboard Clicks—tap the On/Off switch to turn each sound on or off.

Setting the Screen Brightness

The brightness of the iPhone screen determines how well you can see the screen's contents: Generally speaking, the brighter the screen, the easier it is to read. However, the brightness of the iPhone screen also determines how much battery power it drains: The brighter the screen, the more power it consumes.

To control this tradeoff between readability and power consumption, your iPhone comes with an Auto-Brightness feature that automatically adjusts the screen brightness depending on how much surrounding light is available. For example, if the surrounding light is quite bright, it makes the iPhone screen harder to read, so your iPhone automatically brightens the screen to compensate; conversely, if the surrounding light is relatively dim, it makes the iPhone screen easier to read, so your iPhone automatically dims the screen to reduce power consumption.

In some cases, you might prefer to control the brightness of the screen yourself. For example, if you're using your iPhone as an alarm clock, you'll probably want the screen to be quite dim so that it doesn't affect your sleep. Similarly, if you're reading your iPhone in bed, you might want to dim the screen so as not to disturb your spouse. In these cases, you can turn off the Auto-Brightness feature and set the screen brightness by hand.

 LET ME TRY IT

Setting the Screen Brightness

1. In the Home screen, tap Settings. Your iPhone opens the Settings app.

2. Tap Brightness. The Settings app opens the Brightness screen.

3. To prevent your iPhone from controlling the brightness automatically, turn the Auto-Brightness setting to Off.

4. To dim the screen, drag the Brightness slider to the left; for a brighter screen, drag the Brightness slider to the right.

Customizing the iPhone Wallpaper

Wallpaper is an image that appears in the background of the iPhone screen. If you have an iPhone 4 or an iPhone 3GS, you can apply a wallpaper to the Home screen and to the Lock screen (which is the screen that appears when you bring your iPhone out of sleep mode and you have to use the Slide to Unlock control to unlock the phone). You can use 1 of the 26 images that come with your iPhone, or you can use 1 of your own photos.

 LET ME TRY IT

Applying a Predefined Wallpaper

1. In the Home screen, tap Settings to run the Settings app.

2. Tap Wallpaper to open the Wallpaper screen.

3. Tap your current wallpaper images. The Settings app displays a list of photo albums.

4. Tap Wallpaper. The Settings app displays its collection of predefined wallpaper images.

5. Tap the image you want to use. The Settings app displays the Wallpaper Preview screen.

6. Tap Set.

7. Tap the screen (or screens) where you want to apply the wallpaper: Set Lock Screen, Set Home Screen, or Set Both. The Settings app applies the wallpaper.

 **LET ME TRY IT**

Applying a Photo as a Wallpaper

1. In the Home screen, tap Settings to run the Settings app.

2. Tap Wallpaper to open the Wallpaper screen.

3. Tap your current wallpaper images. The Settings app displays a list of photo albums.

4. Tap the photo album that contains the image you want to use. The Settings app displays the album's photos.

5. Tap the image you want to use. The Settings app displays the Move and Scale screen.

6. Drag the photo to position it on the screen the way you want.

7. Set the photo zoom level you want to use by either pinching or spreading your fingers over the photo.

8. Tap Set.

9. Tap the screen (or screens) where you want to apply the wallpaper: Set Lock Screen, Set Home Screen, or Set Both. The Settings app applies the wallpaper.

You can also use the iPhone camera to take a picture and then use it as wallpaper. Open the Camera app take the photo, and then tap the photo thumbnail to open the photo. Tap the Actions button on the left side of the menu bar, and then tap use as Wallpaper.

Configuring the iPhone Keyboard

Your iPhone's onscreen keyboard takes a bit of getting used to, but once you're comfortable with it, you can type accurately and quickly. Even better, your iPhone comes with four keyboard-related settings that can make your keyboard work even easier:

- **Auto-Correction:** This is the feature that automatically corrects your spelling as you type. Leaving this feature on almost always improves the efficiency of most iPhone typists. However, if you find that the corrections are often wrong for you, you can turn it off.

- **Auto-Capitalization:** This feature automatically activates the Shift key when your iPhone detects that you're starting a new sentence (for example, after you've pressed Return, a period, or a question mark). If you find it easier to control capitalization yourself, you can turn off this feature.

- **Enable Caps Lock:** This feature enables you to easily type in all-uppercase letters. Normally, when you tap the Shift key to activate it, your iPhone automatically deactivates the Shift key after you type a single character. This is usually what you want, but if you need to type several characters in a row using only uppercase letters, you should turn on the Enable Caps Lock feature, which enables you to lock the Shift key by double-tapping it.

- **" . " Shortcut:** If you turn on this very useful feature, you can enter a period (.) followed by a single space when you double-tap the spacebar.

 **LET ME TRY IT**

Configuring the iPhone Keyboard

1. In the Home screen, tap Settings. Your iPhone opens the Settings app.

2. Tap General. The Settings app displays the General.

3. Tap Keyboard. The Settings app opens the Keyboard screen.

4. Tap Auto-Correction to turn this feature On or Off.

5. Tap Auto-Capitalization to turn this feature On or Off.

6. Tap Enable Caps Lock to turn this feature On or Off.

7. Tap "." Shortcut to turn this feature On or Off.

Configuring Your iPhone's Sleep Setting

On your iPhone, sleep mode is a power state where your phone is still on but it's using only a minimum amount of battery power because the screen is turned off and your iPhone has temporarily disabled some features (such as the Wi-Fi antenna). You can put your iPhone into sleep mode at any time by pressing the Sleep/Wake button. If your iPhone is on but you're not using it, it will automatically go into sleep mode after two minutes. This is called the Auto-Lock feature, and you can configure it to activate using a different time interval.

 **LET ME TRY IT**

Configuring Your iPhone's Sleep Setting

1. In your iPhone's Home screen, tap Settings to open the Settings app.

2. Tap General to display the General screen.

3. Tap Auto-Lock to display the Auto-Lock screen.

4. Tap the interval you want to use, such as 1 Minute or 5 Minutes.

Protecting Your iPhone with a Passcode Lock

The Auto-Lock setting that you learned about in the previous section "locks" your iPhone only in the sense that it prevents accidental taps while your iPhone is in your pocket, backpack, or purse. However, it's also possible to "lock" your iPhone in the sense of preventing an unauthorized person from using it. You do this by configuring your iPhone with a passcode lock, which is a set of digits or characters that must be entered before your iPhone will awaken from sleep mode. Because iPhones are easily lost or stolen, and because your iPhone contains lots of private and possibly sensitive data, it's a good idea to protect your iPhone with a passcode lock.

Your iPhone supports two kinds of passcode lock:

*   **Simple passcode:** This is a four-digit code, so it's easy to remember, but it might be vulnerable to a determined intruder guessing the passcode.

*   **Complex passcode:** This is a code that uses any combination of letters, numbers, and symbols. To create a strong passcode, make sure it's at least eight characters long and includes characters from at least three of the following four sets: lowercase letters, uppercase letters, numbers, and symbols.

TELL ME MORE   Media 13.3—Protecting Your iPhone

To listen to a free audio recording about protecting your iPhone, log on to my.safaribooksonline.com/9780132182805/media.

LET ME TRY IT

Protecting Your iPhone with a Passcode Lock

1. In the Home screen, tap Settings. Your iPhone opens the Settings app.

2. Tap General. The Settings app displays the General screen.

3. Tap Passcode Lock. The Settings app displays the Passcode Lock screen.

4. If you prefer to set a complex passcode, tap the Simple Passcode switch to Off.

5. Tap Turn Passcode On. The Settings app displays the Set Passcode screen.

6. Tap your passcode. For security purposes, the characters appear in the passcode box as dots.

7. If you're entering a complex passcode, tap Next. The Settings app asks you to reenter the passcode.

8. Tap your passcode again.

9. If you're entering a complex passcode, tap Done.

Whatever you do, do *not* forget your passcode, because if you do you'll be locked out of your phone. If that happens, the only way to get back into your iPhone is to restore it using iTunes. (Connect the iPhone to your computer, click the iPhone in iTunes, and then click Restore.)

Activating Parental Restrictions

If you're giving an iPhone to your young children, or if your children are allowed to use your iPhone, you almost certainly want to protect them from inappropriate content on the Web; on YouTube; and in media, such as music, movies, and apps. You may also want to control whether your children can perform actions such as installing apps and using the camera. Fortunately, your iPhone comes with a set of restrictions that you can activate and that can be overridden only by entering a four-digit passcode.

 **LET ME TRY IT**

Activating Parental Restrictions

1. In the Home screen, tap Settings. Your iPhone opens the Settings app.

2. Tap General. The Settings app displays the General screen appears.

3. Tap Restrictions. The Settings app displays the Restrictions screen.

4. Tap Enable Restrictions. The Settings app displays the Set Passcode screen.

5. Tap the four-digit restrictions passcode and then retype the code. The Settings app returns you to the Restrictions screen and enables all the controls, as shown in Figure 13.4.

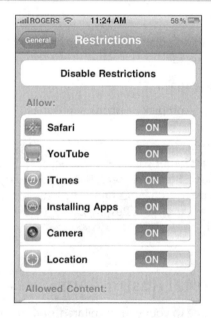

Figure 13.4 *Once you enable restrictions, the Settings app enables all the controls in the Restrictions screen.*

6. In the Allow section, for each app or task that you don't want your children to use, tap its switch to Off.

7. If you don't want your children to make purchases within apps, tap the In-App Purchases switch to Off.

8. Tap Ratings For, tap the country whose ratings you want to use, and then tap Restrictions.

9. For each of the content controls—Music & Podcasts, Movies, TV Shows, and Apps—tap the control and then tap the highest rating you want your children to use.

10. Tap General. The Settings app puts the new restrictions into effect.

index

E

F

G

H

I